M000118883

Wandering 20's

Jan 2019

Kayla —

Thank you so incredibly much for wanting a copy of my book! It truly means the world to me to have your support!

I hope & pray that as you read this, you are able to connect with my story. I hope that it encourages you to look at your own story as well!

I pray that it encourages you to live boldly, feel the feels & to never stop dreaming.

All my love,

Jquen

Wandering 20's

A Journey of Love, Vulnerability, and Dreams

Gwen Debaun

TRILOGY
PROFESSIONAL PUBLISHING MEETS POWERFUL PROMOTION

A wholly owned subsidiary of TBN

Trilogy Christian Publishers A Wholly Owned Subsidiary of Trinity Broadcasting Network2442 Michelle Drive Tustin, CA 92780

Copyright © 2018 by Gwen Debaun

All Scripture quotations, unless otherwise noted, taken from THE HOLY BIBLE, NEW INTERNATIONAL VERSION®, NIV® Copyright © 1973, 1978, 1984, 2011 by Biblica, Inc.® Used by permission of Zondervan. All rights reserved worldwide.

Scripture quotations marked (KJV) taken from The Holy Bible, King James Version. Cambridge Edition: 1769.

All rights reserved, including the right to reproduce this book or portions thereof in any form whatsoever. For information, address Trilogy Christian Publishing Rights Department, 2442 Michelle Drive, Tustin, Ca 92780.

Trilogy Christian Publishing/ TBN and colophon are trademarks of Trinity Broadcasting Network.

For information about special discounts for bulk purchases, please contact Trilogy Christian Publishing.

Manufactured in the United States of America

10 9 8 7 6 5 4 3 2 1

Library of Congress Cataloging-in-Publication Data is available.

ISBN 978-1-64088-163-1

ISBN 978-1-64088-164-8 (ebook)

This book is dedicated to all of those that have stood in my corner and supported me. You are far too numerous and important to leave out. You've helped me grow more than some of you will ever know. You are the true champions, my only hope is that I helped carry on your legacy.

Hey Friend,

I am so happy this book landed in your hands! Perhaps a friend recommended it to you, or maybe it caught your eye on Amazon, or even at a real brick-and-mortar bookstore. However it found its way to you, I am so happy it did.

I want you to know how much I value you and how I much I completely understand where you are in life. Maybe you've got it all figured out, which is amazing; seriously, please tell me your secret! Maybe you're like me, and some days you know exactly what you're doing and why you're doing it and others you don't have even the slightest clue. I want you to know that no matter where you are in life, you are not alone. No matter what your path looks like, especially compared to your best friend or favorite person to follow on IG, it is your path, and it is designed by the only One that matters. ✗

I truly hope you enjoy this book as much as I loved writing it. It's raw; it's real; heck, some of it is straight out of my journals. These past few years of my life have been anything but ordinary. I learned what it's like to live on my own and then come back home. I've learned what it's like to fall in love with a person and a city. I've learned how to come to terms with the way my heart has changed since I was a child. I've learned how I'm not perfect, and I'm never going to be. I've learned what it's like to have my dream job say no, and how to pick myself back up after it seems like everything is against me. I've learned a lot, and my deepest prayer for these words is that they let you learn too, and let you know that you're not alone, wherever you are.

Thank you so much for blessing me with sharing my life with you. I'm praying for you, friend, and I know one day, we'll be able to look back at our lives together and see how they intertwined.

All my best,

—Gwen

Contents

Section One

LOVE

Love.

Love is such a beautiful thing.

Love keeps the soul alive.

Love keeps us wanting to meet people, to find *the one,* and to experience something new.

There are many different kinds of love. I, for one, am an avid believer that love looks different in each aspect of life: from friendships, family, relationships, and the random people whom I connect with on the streets.

Love is a constant in my life. When it seems like the world is spinning faster and I can barely keep my feet underneath me, love is what keeps me going.

One of my first tattoos I got on the instep of my left foot reads: *Love is Infinite.*

Love to me means an array of things. I think of how my parents support me in everything I do. I think of the hugs I get from my nieces that would thaw even the harshest of winters. I think of my best friends who bring me food or coffee, or even pay for my meal when we go out. I think of the sunrises and sunsets that can make my heart sing. I think of those first sips of coffee on a cold spring morning (right as the sun is rising), and the whole day is still ahead. That's love to me. An array of different things. Some so simple, others as complex as DNA.

Love means all these things and more. The reason I chose to have "Love" tattooed on my foot for the rest of my life is because love is a part of me and my story. Life is full of peaks and valleys; how we respond to those peaks and valleys defines us. For me, struggles are what have helped define how I love. ★

Though my history would not show up on *America's Most Wanted,* it isn't all rainbows and butterflies.

Growing up, I was a gossiper and a liar.

There I said it, and it's true. I would say or do anything to be friends with someone. You could also say that I didn't have a spine, that I didn't think for myself, that I did what everyone else was doing.

I wanted to be a part of the 'cool kids,' and I would agree with the rumors they started about the girl in class; heck, I would even help spread the rumors. It took me awhile and some hard conversations for my little grade-school heart to realize the damage that being a gossiper could do. I hurt friends, teachers, people I didn't even know I could hurt; all for the sake of 'making friends'.

When I wasn't gossiping about others, chances are I was fabricating some kind of tale to tell my friends, teachers, or even my parents. Some were small, like claiming I had brushed my teeth before bed when I truly hadn't; others were larger, like blaming something that happened in class or at home on a classmate or my brother. As I got older, I stopped lying as I realized the consequences of what I was doing. Someone else was getting in trouble for spreading that rumor that I had helped spread. My brother was getting in trouble for my little white lie. I realized that I couldn't keep gossiping and lying to get what I wanted. That doesn't mean that I flipped a switch and completely stopped cold turkey. There were times when I still gossiped, when the taste of hearing all the juicy news about a classmate was too sweet for me to ignore and then share with my friends. There were times when telling a small lie helped me not get in trouble, until it came back around.

But something started to change in me, something that was bigger than my want to stay out of trouble or even my want to know everything that was going on; it was my want to stop. My want was to change my heart and my natural tendencies to lie or to share someone else's news. I thought about it, really thought about what I was doing; gossiping, lying, you name it, how could someone still love me? How could I love those that I was spreading rumors about, badmouthing, lying to?

I realized that someone did love me. Someone loved me even though I did all these things. Someone cared about me so deeply that He would do anything for me. So why didn't I love Him?

I started to learn about Jesus.

I'm not here to shove religion down your throat. Some of you who are reading this and see the name "Jesus" are instantly going to close this book, put it back wherever you found it, and walk away. I really hope you don't do that.

Not that I'm trying to convert you, but I think there's a *reason* you picked this is up, and I think you might learn something if you let yourself.

As I got older and started to realize the repercussions of what I was doing, the effects of the rumors I was spreading about others, and the way that I was treating people, I also started to learn more about Jesus.

Jesus loved those who spread rumors about Him, He loved those who plotted His demise, He loved the leper, the woman having the affair, the liar, the doubter, the proud. He loved *everyone*. It blew my mind.

Here's Jesus who hung out with those who were sick, hurting, and prideful and *loved* them. He loved them so much that He came to Earth, lived a sinless life, and then died in the most painful way imaginable so that we, you and I and everyone we meet, would be able to have eternal life in Heaven. That's how much He loves us. He loves us just as we are; just as sick, hurting, dirty and prideful that I was, I am. He loved me.

He *loves* me.

Jesus loves me even when I make a mistake. He loves me even when I give into the sweet taste of gossip. He loves me even when I curse. He loves me even when I tell a little white lie. He loves me through my best and my worse. There is not limit on His love for us. Which means there is no limit on love.

There is truly no limit on how much you can love someone. There are different kinds of love for a reason. You can love someone as a brother and another as a soul mate. You can love someone as a teammate and another as grandparent.

There is just no limit because love is infinite.

Chapter One
The Auntie

I love my family. They are my everything. Growing up they weren't my favorite people to hang out with, but as I have grown older, I have found I truly cherish the time we get to spend together.

Something changes when your siblings decide to start a family of their own. It's different. They change, and you love the crazy kids they make.

My brother, Noah, and his wife, Sara, have three wonderful, little girls.

I remember when my oldest niece was born. I had just turned 19 literally two days beforehand. We were in the hospital waiting not-so-patiently for her to arrive. I was working on getting ready for my first semester of college, and I had just come home from a retreat on campus that helped prepare me for school. I was *tired*. I was falling asleep in the waiting room, and every few minutes a chime rang over the intercom saying another baby was born.

At 19, I wasn't really a fan of babies. They weren't all that cute, they smelled, they spit up, they couldn't do anything for themselves. They looked like a mixture of aliens and old people. My views haven't since changed much, but we'll get to that later.

Here I am, a 19-year-old, sitting with my family in the waiting room. The parents were taking turns going in and out of the room checking on Noah and Sara, seeing what they needed. Eventually, it was decided that my little niece would arrive to the world via C-section. We all sat in the waiting room, anxiously waiting to hear the chime that was hers to tell us she was here. It came, and we all waited for my brother to come out and tell us all was well.

He came in his scrubs, and we followed him like little ducklings into their room. There she was, my first niece, Infinity Adonai, lying asleep in her little buggy.

My heart swelled when I laid eyes on her. She was this pink, wrinkly ball of wonder. I knew right then that I would do anything for her.

The moment I met my second niece is a bit of a different story.

She was born in Chicago while I was in Washington, DC doing an internship. The weeks leading up to her birth, I was trying with all my might to find a way to get to Chicago to meet her. My parents had driven up from Indy, and it seemed like everyone was there, helping and celebrating her awaited birth. We didn't know if she was a boy or a girl until she arrived.

I, unfortunately, couldn't find a way to make it up. I had class and work, and the price of a last-minute ticket was much too steep on my college-student budget.

The day of her birth, I was in the office glued to my phone wanting updates. I texted Noah, Sara, Mom, and Dad all wanting to know what was going on. If they didn't text back within five minutes, I texted again and texted someone else. I *needed* to know what was happening.

I'm not the most patient person in the world, I should let you know. So as I was sitting not-so-patiently in the office 600 miles away from the birth of my second niece, I thought I would go crazy waiting to hear what was happening.

Finally, I got the news: Abigail Rose had arrived.

I was an auntie to two.

I got some photos of her cuteness and couldn't help but "ooh" and "aww" over her wrinkling little fingers and toes, and sweet baby cheeks.

Her baby photos were the background of my computer until I made it home for Thanksgiving. Everyone I would see would have to suffer through seeing her photos. Weeks later when I finally got home for the holidays and got to see her in person, my heart melted once more.

Much like her sister, I knew I would do anything to make her smile, to make her happy.

The summer of 2017 my third niece was born, Miriam Josephine.

I took the day off work in anticipation, just in case my nieces wanted to see their auntie, or Noah and Sara needed someone to run errands for them.

We went over to the hospital to meet them in the evening after she had arrived. Noah was tired and had a sappy look of happiness on his face, Sara was sore, sleepy and excited; they both were hungry. And there she was, little Miri. A bundle of pink much like her sisters were, wrapped up in blankets so that you could only see her button nose.

The next day when I brought food to help keep Noah and Sara entertained, I sat down on the couch and held her. She was so, so small. She fit perfectly in the crook of my arm and just laid there. I felt it once more: my heart pulsed faster at the sight of her sleeping in my arms, her little tiny face, eyes closed, mouth slightly open, her long, slender fingers curled under her chin. I would do anything for her.

My nieces are much older now, Infinity goes by "Finn" and is five years old now, Abigail goes by "Rose" and is four, and Miri is just a few months old. They have the sweetest personalities in the world, and are all so vastly different. Finn loves dance, and Rose loves animals. They both love the color pink and musicals. Finn loves cake, and Rose loves icing. At the moment they are both enthralled with fairies and princesses, but this is subject to change on the day I see them.

I've had my fair share of time away from them. The first time I left was for an 11-month mission trip. My little ladybugs didn't really know what was going on, but they knew I would come back.

I missed their hugs more than I thought possible. Holding them in my arms is the sweetest place in the world.

When I came home from my trip and more recently when I came home from an internship, all I wanted was their hugs.

Have you ever had a hug from someone and it just felt right to be in their arms? ✈

That is what it feels like with them. There is no sweeter place.

When they come running, screaming "AUNTIE!!" and plow into my arms, I am at my happiest. They are the sweetest little girls on the planet, and I would do anything for them.

Their "I love yous" are the best in the world. They look at you with wide eyes, smiles, and it honestly feels like my heart will explode. I finally understand what the Grinch must have felt like looking down at Whoville. There are days where we are playing *Clue* or *Jenga* or coloring fairies and princesses, and then amid all of the fun and games, one of them will whisper, "Auntie."

"Yes, sweetie," I'll respond.

"I love you," they'll say.

And in those moments, my heart grows three sizes. All is right in the world.

It is in these moments, I also realize how deeply in love with these three girls I am. Part of being the Auntie means I get the fun role. I'm the one who gets to play and laugh, and there aren't too many rules. Whenever I take care of them, I only have two rules: Don't be dumb, and don't hurt yourself, me, or your sister.

While being fun is entertaining, one of the hardest parts about being an Auntie is that I would give them the world if I could.

Especially when they say, "I love you, Auntie," I realize how much I love them back. There are days when all they want to do is have me watch them dance. I'll do it. I'll sit there for hours and watch them parade after one another spinning and twirling like little ballerinas.

There are times when they just want me to color with them, or more accurately pick the color that they should use and show them where to color with it.

There are times when they just want a piece of cake or some ice cream, and I would get it for them if I had it. Unfortunately, I usually don't, and more unfortunately, Noah and Sara don't like to give them lots of sweets.

Part of being the auntie and not being their parent is that my role is vastly different. I can be fun all the time, it's my responsibility almost to make sure my time with them is spent with endless giggles and hugs and fun. I get to do what I want to do for them. My part as the auntie, part of my love for them, makes me not have a spine.

I know that my spine will come with time and just wanting them to be happy, but for now, I am the world's biggest invertebrate when it comes to them, and I have no shame in saying it.

I would give them the world and more if I could. But most importantly, I just want them to be happy. ★

Chapter Two
Family

I was raised by some of the best parents ever. I might be a little biased since they are *my* parents but seriously, here's a few reasons as to why.

My parents have *always* loved me. ✗

My parents loved me when I wanted to paint my room and proceeded to get more paint on the floor than on my walls. My walls are four different colors if that gives you any idea.

My parents loved me when my brother and I rollerbladed in the kitchen and hallway and would ram into the cabinets and doors.

My parents loved me when my brother and I would get into fights.

My parents loved me when I would practice volleyball on the side of the house right by their room even while they were napping.

My parents loved me and Noah when we would play soccer in the family room, practice tennis against the walls, and build a fort with sheets and staples.

My parents loved me when I got sick in high school and couldn't go to school.

My parents loved me when I did something stupid like wrecked a car.

My parents loved me when I got 1350 on the SAT (this was when it was out of 2400).

My parents loved me when I wanted to intern in DC for a semester.

My parents loved me when I wanted to take a gap year and do mission work.

My parents love me to this day, a part-time employed 24-year-old who still lives at home.

Now just like anyone's parents, mine are a bit odd. They have always and will always love me, but just like my friends, they show love in many different ways.

My dad, the engineer, shows love in the weirdest of ways to me. I am a touchy, feely individual, and quality time and talking are my love languages. My dad is a man of few words but incredibly wise nonetheless. My dad loves to give gifts, *his kind* of gifts to others. For years growing up I would get these old books that he thought I would like or find interesting. One year, I was really into Astronomy so he got me an Astronomy textbook from the 1970s. I didn't like it. Heck, I probably said, "Umm thanks Dad." because I didn't understand his intentions behind it.

See to him, the book said, "Here's a book on Astronomy since you're interested in it. It may be a bit old, but it holds a lot of information, and I would like to read it with you."

Whereas to me, the book said, "Here's an old, used textbook from the Stone Ages. I hope you enjoy."

Two different things that one book says.

As I got older though, I began to try to appreciate his kinds of gifts from the random thirty-plus-year-old books that I'm sure hold some kind of knowledge that I can acquire, to the CDs and movies from that one artist or actor that I said I liked at that one point in time.

He remembers, which is the sweetest, and he means well, which is all that matters.

Here's the cool thing about my dad: he will do *anything* for anyone. Family, friend, stranger, he'll do it. He'll help them in any way he possibly can. My dad is one of those people who just gives without a second thought.

My freshman year in college, I was in the middle of a major study session, it was right before midterms, and I was swamped with assignments. My friend Kierstin and I were studying in my dorm, and my parents texted me to see how we were doing. I mentioned how hungry we were and how much we wanted Mexican food. About an hour later I got a call from my dad saying that he was in the parking lot with food.

During one of the first breaks of college, I came home, and all my friends and I were heading to the movies. As a college freshman, I was loving my freedom of not being at home, so when I came back, it was a hard transition of staying out late, getting midnight coffee and tacos with friends, to being home where your parents go to bed at 9pm.

As I was heading down the stairs, my parents were in the kitchen finishing up dinner and asked when I might be home, and I told them probably late. We were getting food and seeing a movie and then maybe just hanging out. My dad came down the hall as I was putting on my shoes and gave me $20 bill and said, "Have fun with your friends!"

I stood there, having put on both shoes, and said, "Thanks Dad, but I don't need it, I have money." As I tried to hand it back.

My dad responded, walking back down the hall into the kitchen, "I know, but you're home, which means we take care of you." With that, I left for the movies with a fresh, crisp $20 bill in my pocket, in awe of my parents' generosity.

I'll never forget one of my hardest semesters in college. I was trying to take both chemistry and biology along with my other classes. I was interested in both, but they were kicking my butt with the amount of math and work that was required of them. As finals week drew nearer, I drew more frustrated and concerned with what my grades would look like at the end of the term.

One day, I went to go check my mail, and I had a card from my dad. It was a card full of encouragement. For a man of few words, he picked the perfect card, encouraging me not to quit even when it gets hard. Telling me it is going to be ok, that the view after I trudged through the valley was going to be so worth it.

I still have this card, all these years later. It sits on my desk, right next to some flowers. I pick it up occasionally; just to read the front, *Don't Quit*. And when I need that extra boost, I open it again and read the message inside.

My dad is always going to be there for me, no matter how many squabbles we have, and no matter how many tattoos I have that he doesn't approve of. He is always in my corner, supporting me, loving me.

My mom is my best friend.

My mom is one of those people who when you first meet them treats you like their own; their own family, their own children. My friends often joke about how my parents are their second parents, and vise versa, but it really is true.

Growing up no matter how many friends I brought over, my mom would work tirelessly in the kitchen making batches of waffles and cookies for us to all munch on.

She is the kind of woman that you grow up wanting to be. She is kind, thoughtful, joyous, intelligent, a friend, a mother, a confidant, an encourager; and an all-around wondrous human being. While she may not know just how incredible she is, she's my mom, and I will forever love and appreciate her and all she does for me.

Growing up, my mom would dote on me; I'm the youngest, and I love it. She encouraged me to focus on my art; she loved it when I wanted to paint my room many colors (asked me often if I was sure but in the end knew it would be ok). She loved my friends. She loved it when my brother and I would venture out into the backyard and go on adventures between the trees. She encouraged us to be kids.

Even as I've gotten older, she encourages me to do everything I want to do. Of course, if she had her way, I would stay close to home, far enough that she and my dad have to drive to come and see me, but close enough that it's still in the same zip code. But she knows that that way of living isn't what my life is supposed to be like.

When I came to her crying, unsure of what I wanted to do, but knowing that I was meant to take a gap year from college and do mission work, she was scared and nervous for me. *Would you go back to school? Why can't this wait until you graduate? Why now? Are you sure this is what God is calling you to do?*

Even though I couldn't answer all of those questions right then and there, when the time came for me to start preparing to go, she supported me.

She's supported all of my crazy decisions: deciding to go to college, even though the doctors weren't sure if I could, spending a semester in Washington, DC, going on the World Race, and more, She has supported me through it all.

My mom is my biggest cheerleader, and she loves me through and through.

I could go on for days of all the times she has supported me, even when she maybe didn't want to, but she knew I needed it.

You see my mom, much like me, has a heart for everyone. When anything goes wrong in someone's life, she is right there, holding their hand through it. She lets them know they can come over, get a cup of tea, a warm meal, anything. She is there to help.

My parents, God love them, it's not easy being my parents. I can be stubborn, bull-headed, and sometimes my feet are miles off the ground with how much I am dreaming. But my parents still love me. Even when we fight about the smallest of things, I know that they still love me and they want what is best for me.

I didn't realize until a few days ago, but I want what is best for them. I want the world to know how amazing they are. I want to shout it from the rooftops, build them a castle, make a fund in their name for some child someday who just wants to live an amazing life. They deserve the world, if only I could give it to them.

My brother and I were a handful to my parents growing up. As my mom's hair started to turn grey (or sparkly as we prefer to call it), she would grab a strand and tell us the story of how she got it.

This is from when you and your brother decided that you wanted to go sledding. But not outside because it was too cold, and there wasn't any snow on the ground, but instead go sledding down the stairs in laundry baskets and then plow into the wall.

This one is from when you two decided at 7PM one night that you were going to trade rooms, again! A week after you had just changed rooms! You both brought all of your stuff out into the hallway and you, Gwen, slept with me and your dad because you couldn't move it all back into your room before bedtime.

These stories always make me laugh. My brother and I were mischievous little children. We still are, we just get away with a bit more now.

Growing up, my brother and I weren't always the best of friends. I was his kid sister as he got older which meant I was annoying. (To my defense, I probably really was as annoying as he claimed. I liked to bug to him, but it was for the best of reasons, I just wanted to know what he was doing.)

As Noah got older, he got wiser. It was nice when I was in high school and even made it to college to *finally* have a cool, older brother who wanted to spend time with me and get to know me. He was married, and his wife was sweet and fun. They liked to FaceTime me at school. It was nice; it was something I had always wanted.

My brother is always there for me, much like my parents. There were times when I would call him and ask him questions, and he would help me work through any kind of situation. I would call with study questions, friend questions, how-to-get-a-job questions. All of them, and he would always give me some kind of advice. His advice usually consisted of me making the right decision in the long term: *What would provide the best thing for you later on?*

This is something that I equally love and hate about my brother, just how different we are. To him, the world is black and white. To me the world is an endless array of colors and ideas.

To him, it's a simple *yes or no.*

To me, it's a *yes, no, sorta, maybe, kinda, possibly.*

We clash, more now I think as we have gotten older. At first when I realized Noah saw things in black and white, I was really confused. *How could someone who grew up in the same house I did only see things this way and not understand my way?*

Then I realized how wonderful that is. If my brother saw the world the same way I do, it would only be helpful when it comes to a discussion if I wanted to come to the *same* conclusion. But how boring is that? We would never offer up the other side. We would never be able to come to a conclusion that maybe there isn't just one way, maybe there's more. We wouldn't just be able to say "okay" and leave it; we would be able to consider the possibility of there being something else.

This is what I love most about my brother. No matter how much his viewpoints annoy the hell out of me, he helps me grow. It's as simple as that.

Chapter Three

Marriage

Growing up I never wanted to get married, let alone have a boyfriend. I *yess* prided myself in my independence. One of the reasons why I never wanted to, short of never wanting to leave my parents, is because I thought the only way marriage worked was how my parents displayed theirs.

I didn't want a marriage like my parents. One that fought. One that had money problems. One that didn't always see eye to eye. I didn't want that, so I didn't think that I wanted a marriage.

As my brother became a husband, he showed me that their example isn't what marriage *has* to look like.

When Noah got married, I still didn't want a marriage. I couldn't understand why someone would willingly decide to spend the rest of their lives' with someone else. Like hello, you *really* have to *love* that person. What if you got mad or upset or you found that they had this crazy annoying quirk and there was nothing that you could do about it? Or worse, what if they didn't like coffee or pancakes? You were stuck with them. It just didn't make sense.

Noah and Sara are by no means perfect. They fight, they have their struggles just like my parents do. But when they got married, I was able to see something differently. It probably helped that I wasn't thirteen anymore; I was eighteen and learning the ways of the world.

When I saw Noah and Sara so happy together, I realized that that is what a marriage looks like, being happy with the person who is by your side.

I see it now, with my parents. And when I look hard enough in my past, I see those moments of love between my parents, and they shine brighter than before, almost like a veil was lifted.

There were moments where my parents just looked at one another, across the room or across the dinner table, and it was a look so full of love that one could only believe that they were perfect together. It was the tender moments of when my dad randomly brings home flowers for my mom, and I put them in a vase. It was the moments where my mom makes sure to get the exact kind of soda that my dad likes. It was the moments where when mom is putting away dinner and she makes my dad's lunch for the next day as well. The days when my dad drives us around shopping, getting gas, and will even pick up and drop my mom off at work because she doesn't really like to drive. It's the moments when they're sitting on the same side of the booth when we're out laughing and smiling at each other while sharing food.

The times when Noah and Sara dance, sing, and kiss little Finn in their studio apartment. It's the times when Noah makes dinner and Sara makes dessert. It's the times when Sara calls Noah on his drive home just to say "hi" and "I love you." It's the times when Noah falls asleep on the couch and Sara covers him with a blanket. It's the moments when Noah picks up Sara's drink at Starbucks and brings it home. When Noah gets up earlier than usual just to make her and the girls breakfast. It's the moments when Noah shares his last piece of waffle with Sara.

These are the moments of marriage that I love and make me realize that my mindset as a child was so defined by what I saw when I was younger.

These are the moments I look to with joy, happiness, love, and hope.

No matter how many issues my parents have, no matter how many squabbles they get into, they still love each other. Because love is something stronger that binds them together forever.

Chapter Four

Where You Are

I have spent much of life wanting to be in the next chapter of it. yes

I remember growing up and being in middle school and dreaming of high school. Then as high school rolled around, I dreamed of college. When college happened, I dreamt of what I was going to do when I left. Now that I have graduated college, I haven't stopped dreaming about what I want to do, but my dreams have changed.

I've always been looking towards something else, wanting to do the next thing. If I do this, then I'll develop this kind of mentality. I was always reaching towards the next goal without enjoying where I was.

Let's recap my last five years really quickly:

In 2012, I graduated high school, and my best friend and I took a road trip down to Florida to celebrate. My first niece was born that summer too. I was able to attend a retreat on campus before starting my first year of college. My first year was a whirlwind! I ended up getting a concussion right before Thanksgiving and had to have my appendix out the day after Christmas. Super fun ways to remember my freshman year of college. But that year, I also started working in coffee, which has changed my life.

When classes ended in the spring of 2013, I started working multiple jobs to save up for my semester in Washington, DC where I was going to be doing an internship. In August, my parents and I drove out there, and I got settled into my first apartment. It was an amazing semester of growth, friendship, and learning. As the internship ended, and I headed back home to Indy, I moved into my new dorm room to start the spring semester of 2014. It was a hard transition coming from working a 40-hour work week and classes to just taking classes, but I learned so much while I was in the District that I wanted to excel just as much back home.

As summer rolled around, I was determined to catch up on my coursework, and enrolled in summer courses. I even stayed on campus to make it easier. When classes began again in the fall of 2014, I was working three jobs on campus and one off campus. I wanted to save money and was also working in a few different fields to see what I was really interested in. The fall of 2014 was a major time of transition. I began to look into mission programs to embark on and take time away from school. I found one and started to fundraise, and before I knew it January rolled around and I was off on my first-ever, long-term mission trip, the World Race.

2015 was a year stock full of memories. It was a year where I grew more confident in myself and the Lord. Many of the lessons I have learned can be found in these pages. When I came home from the Race in November of 2015, I started working at a local coffee shop to save money and get my feet under me again. I also started taking classes again the following January. Much like the summer two years before, I took three summer courses to be able to graduate in December 2016. Following my graduation I started my dream internship with an organization called Thirst Project. When my internship came to a close, I came back home with absolutely no idea as to what I was doing; just the knowledge that home was where I needed to be.

You see, when I look at all that I've been blessed to do, I see how everything was so beautifully aligned by God that I don't doubt why I am back home right now. I also see all these amazing opportunities that I was blessed enough to have. Not many people can say that at 23, they have traveled the continental United States and the world; but I have and I hope to some more.

One of the things that has been hard for me to learn was just to be able to be happy where I am and not to long for what else there is in the future. When we focus so much on what is to come, we lose sight of the beautiful things that are happening right beneath our feet. We lose sight of seeing springtime, the trees beginning to bloom, getting greener every day. The tulips that are planted at the side of my house, for years I would walk past them on my way inside; I would drive down my street and out onto the main road with one main goal: *get to work on time.* Now, I am able to drive more slowly and more cautiously. I look at my neighbor's houses, some have changed dramatically over the years, and others are still the same as I remember as a child.

Being the frantic Hurricane Gwendolyn that my parents called me when I was little was wonderful for much of my growing up years. It allowed me to have many experiences that I will treasure forever, even some that I've yet to fully understand. But from having been a hurricane to now a steady stream, I am able to say on this side of the storm that it's better sometimes to live day to day.

When I came home from the World Race, an eleven-month mission trip to eleven different countries, I realized just how much of my time I spent in the wonders of *"why"*. I wanted to know *why* God had called me onto the World Race. *Why* I had spent a year of my life traveling and spreading the love of the Lord. I didn't really understand the *why*, the purpose of it all.

When I got home, my life was vastly different than what it had been. I had been living out of a backpack, and now I had a closet.

I had been throwing away my toilet paper, and now I could flush it.

I had been taking bucket showers and watching how much water I used, and now I had faucets galore.

I had walked most places and always had a buddy, and suddenly the roads in my town were meant for driving, not for walking. And most people had other things to do than accompany me to the store.

Everyone spoke the same language too, and everyone was almost always in this hurry to get to the next place.

When I came home, I realized I needed to change the way I was looking at things. I needed to stop wondering *why* in the world I was back home and not back on the field somewhere. Most importantly, I needed to look at each day as its own and find the *magic in the mundane.*

For me, it was (and sometimes is) so easy to just long for the future. Even still I wonder, *God why am I back home? What is here that I am supposed to do? Why have I done all these things to just come right back here? What is the purpose of this?*

And even though I haven't figured it out yet, I've realized some really important things.

When you slow down, you realize that life is more than waking up, working, coming home, and sleeping. Life is a mixture of these beautiful moments that take you by surprise.

The moments when you walk into work and strike up a conversation with a customer, one who loves adventures, coffee and Jesus just as much as you.

The moments where you're driving and decide to roll your windows down and blast your music with the wind in your hair and the sun on your face, and you feel as though anything is possible.

The moments where you decide to take your friend out to lunch, and you get to see where she works and what exactly she does.

The moments where you take food over to your friend's house, and you guys have a pasta pitch-in and sit there until 2 am drinking wine and talking about life.

The moments where you decide to take a different exit to go home, just to see something that you don't usually see.

The moments where you really savor each sip of your coffee rather than gulping it down to get the day started.

The moments where your nieces are climbing all over you like you're a jungle gym, laughing, giggling, kicking you sometimes, but you see their smile and you're not thinking about what homework assignments you have due, who you need to text back, when you need to leave to get to work. You're thinking about them, their love for you and your love for them, and how when they hug you, time stands still.

These are the moments that I long for. These are the moments that I love. These are the moments that I am seeking in this season of Rest. Even though at times my heart may long for a different place, my feet are here. And I truly am learning to love where I am rather than where I want to be.

Chapter Five
Mountain Tops

Have you ever realized how much easier it is to love life when everything is going well? Like when you're getting dressed in the morning and your favorite outfit is clean in your closet waiting to be worn, and it fits just perfectly. Then when you get to work, everyone is in amazing moods, and every customer who comes in is happy, thoughtful, and kind. You never once grow hungry or tired because you're able to take your breaks when you need them. There's no drama going on with your friends or your family. Everything just seems perfect?

Yeah, it doesn't happen very often that everything falls perfectly into place and life goes smoothly, because, well, it's life. But oftentimes I find myself loving life more when it is going smoothly; when I get enough sleep, have a good work and life balance, you know, the small things. When life isn't going well, it's not because everything just up and decided to not work out, but it's usually the little things that seem to not be going well.

There is this amazing song by Ben Rector called "I Like You" that really seems to put those big and small moments into perspective for me. When I first heard it, I thought it was an adorable love song. The second time I heard it, this one line stood out above the rest

'Cause life is more than the mountain tops, it's the walking in between,

and I like you walking next to me.

Wow. Powerful, right?

As you can see from my timeline, only the big moments stand out: the jobs, the internships, the starting classes. What you don't see is during those times I was doing and learning so much more than just those highlights.

I don't want to be 90 years old, sitting on the porch, talking with my great-grandkids about the major highlights. Have you ever seen the show *How I Met Your Mother?* If you haven't, you should. It's a hilariously cute show, but to give you a bit of a scoop on it:

Ted, the main character, is telling the story of how he met his kids' mother, not just the big moments, but the *everything*. Each day of however many years it takes to meet the love of his life. *Every single detail.*

I am sure my great-grandkids would hate it if I told them every single detail, but I want to be able to remember them.

It's not just the big moments that shape our lives, it's the everything. The decision to get a coffee at a shop rather than making it at home. The choice of which route to take on your way home.

Everything.

I have this tattoo of an arrow on my right index finger. It's a wonderful reminder to me to keep going.

Here's the thing about arrows, they can't move forward without first moving backwards.

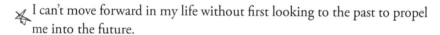 I can't move forward in my life without first looking to the past to propel me into the future.

Even though the highlights, the bullet points, and the major moments are what help us define our lives, it's all the little things that have happened in our past that help mold our future.

Chapter Six

Loved & Lost

Have you ever looked back on your life and thought about who you had a crush on? 🏹

Every once in awhile my friends and I will look back at old yearbooks, or something will pop into our minds that will remind us of old crushes. When we do this, we all just have to laugh at how we used to be. Some of these guys were incredibly kind, great human beings, and some not so much. While some of them were not the best to hang around, especially romantically. But if we weren't able to look back and laugh about who we liked, I think we would just be too set in our ways. Here's to you guys, the lost boys of my life.

My First Real Crush

I met you at church. Which in my book at the time, meant you were a winner. I thought you were the perfect, young gentleman. You were friendly, you asked me about my friends and about my family. But there was something off about you. You only reached out when you wanted to. I don't blame you for anything; honest, I'm happy with the way things ended, and I'm happy you're happy. I'll remember you always as one of the first guys to hold the door open for me. As the guy who asked if he could sit next to me at church. As the guy who was my first real crush.

The One that Found His One

We met my senior year of high school. You were everything and more that I could have hoped for in a friend, let alone a boyfriend. We had similar taste in music, food, and extracurricular activities. You were a prize to all of my friends. Everyone knew your name, not in the popular jock way, but in the "he's a good guy" way. I didn't want to start anything, I thought high school is high school, and I'll be off at college in the fall. But you know what? You stuck with me. I remember that summer before college when we went hiking together. Sometimes it was just the two of us, and other times we had other friends there. We talked about everything under the sun: school, God, family, friends, relationships, marriage, travel, kids. You name it, and we talked about it. It was perfect. You were perfect.

I remember when I would come home from breaks, and we would get to hang out. And then that one time I said those three fateful words: "I like you." And our perfect friendship shattered. I didn't see you for a while, and man it was rough. You were my best friend, and then you were gone. A year went by, and finally one of us reached out. You gave me advice on my travels and helped me with some gear. You told me about a girl you'd met over the summer. I knew it before you said it: "She's the one." I was hurt, but you never would have known. I was hoping against hope that you were mine. Even though I knew you weren't. Want to know something crazy? When I saw your wedding photos, and we started talking when I came home on breaks from college, I was so happy for you and knew that she really was your "One" and you were hers. You two fit so perfectly together, it was undeniable.

Here's to you, the one that found his one. I am so happy for you, happier still that we can be friends. You two are truly perfect together.

The Older Guy

I met you my freshman year of college. I thought you were the coolest guy there was in our friend group. You were older, and there was something unsure about you that I was really intrigued by. What I didn't love was how many girls it seemed like you were always talking to. Most of our friends were the same, so when I would hang out with them, and you weren't there, another girl was always talking about you. It was a different girl each time too. Yet, you and I were still talking.

I remember when we first really hung out. We went hiking, do you remember? I'm sorry. I probably should have said that a long time ago. I saw your face when you were helping me over a ridge, and I knew I didn't really feel that way about you, the way that you did about me. I was a jerk that day; that one really is on me. When I brought up the guy back home I was into, I was being a jerk. My plan, if you will, was to get us to just stay friends, but it completely backfired with you. You seemed to cut me out after that. When we started talking again, I was really happy. You were such a great friend when you wanted to be. I started to wonder if maybe there was something more between us, if it could even be possible. Then you told me about your girlfriend, and that's right about when we stopped talking again. You know what's funny about you though? I was always there, and I always will be. I told you I have an open door to everyone, you just have to knock and come in. ★

That's exactly what you did when you two broke up. I was still here for you, but not in the way you wanted. I didn't want to be used; I just wanted to be your friend.

Now, you're with another girl, and it's been years since we really talked. I really am happy for you. I'm happier still that I realized I don't want a guy who only wants me when he doesn't have someone else. I want a guy who wants me all the time.

Just Not Right

We met freshman year, but it wasn't until I was leaving for my internship in Washington, DC that we really started to be friends. While I was gone, you became friends with one of my best friends, who was like a brother to me. When I came home, it seemed too perfect. You were friends with all of mine, and we hung out all the time. You were always there. You asked questions, you challenged me, and you were just there.

I'll never forget when we were both working on homework for different classes, and you would look up and ask one of the most philosophical questions I had ever heard. Then we would proceed to spend an hour (that precious hour that we should have been doing homework) debating it. I loved it.

As the days passed, and our mutual friend transferred to a different school, we tried to stay friends. We really did. But we were just a bit too different. We wanted different things. We thought so differently. But I loved our time together. You grew me. I don't know if you knew that, but you did. You grew me so much that semester. Our talks really helped shape the way that I think now. Whether you were playing devil's advocate, or you simply wanted to broaden your mind with a discussion, you helped me see even more colors in the world than what I already did. I know you'll be the perfect guy for someone one of these days; you're a keeper for sure. I'm sorry you're not mine. I would have loved it, but it just wasn't right.

Maybe In a Different Life

When we first met, I had just started working at a coffee shop and had just come home from the World Race. In all the nicest of ways, I was a mess. I was home and didn't understand life at home. I was starting up school and was terrified. You were there. You would come in, and we would talk for hours about everything: life, family, friends, dreams, hope, money, God, relationships. Absolutely everything, nothing was off limits with us. When our friendship grew beyond me behind the espresso bar, I realized just how much I cared for you. You helped me out, you wanted to get to know me, you were amazing. I know we both wanted something, what that something was, I don't know if we'll ever know. Perhaps we wanted something to work out between us even if we knew it would never work out. Perhaps we just didn't want to go there for fear that there were too many things that didn't add up. I'm not sure either of us will ever know.

When I came home this last time and got to see you, my heart swelled. Here you are my friend. Four hours went by with us chatting over coffee, and it honestly felt like just a few minutes. You bent your listening ear to hear my stories and struggles. I bent mine to give advice and help. You're always going to be there for me, and I'm always here for you.

I realized when I saw you that you're not mine to keep forever, maybe in a different life it would work, and you would be mine. But for now, you're not. Selfishly I want to keep you all to myself—you're amazing, you know—but I just can't. I have to share you with the world so they can experience your awesomeness too.

Always There

My friends knew it before I did, I liked you. When I told a few of them before I left for my internship, they laughed and said "Duh! Are you just now realizing this?" I really was. I wasn't leaving to find someone or fall for someone; I was leaving for something greater than that. I didn't want you to be my focus while I was gone. I didn't want to get distracted. I put so many boundaries up in my mind for when I finally met you in person, but when I saw you walking toward me at baggage claim, I just knew you would always be in my life. Your hugs, oh my gosh your hugs, are one of my favorite places in the world. You should get an award for them.

You remember when we were trying to work in the spare office and somehow we just got to talking about life for like three hours? I do. You asked some amazing questions. I laughed so hard when you didn't know what RBF (resting female dog face) was. We bonded over our hate for being woken up and our love for coffee and adventure. I knew you were the perfect teammate.

When everything changed, I was devastated. I thought I was going to be losing one of my best friends. Luckily I didn't. You say everything happens for a reason; this one I think is so that we would be better friends afterwards. While we were on the road, you were my crutch sometimes. You helped me and kept me sane. I don't know what I would have done without you.

When I saw you in that random city and got a hug from you again, I was so happy. Delirious with lack of sleep, but all I could see was your face and smile. When we spent hours driving together, I couldn't have been happier.

I didn't know if I was going to tell you, but I'm so glad that I did. You're one of my best friends, my forever teammate. As we stood there in the hallway, your arms wrapped around me, I didn't want to move. I wanted to stay there forever.

When you called a few days ago, I couldn't believe I was hearing your voice. It seemed so far away but so close. I missed it. I miss you. I don't know if anything will ever happen between us. Part of me craves it, and another part of me doesn't want to risk losing you. But I know that you are always there, no matter the distance, no matter the time, you are always there.

Chapter Seven
Friends

My friends are amazing. Seriously. If you have the honor of meeting them, you would love them just as much as I do.

I have had the honor of knowing some of my friends for over a decade, and others just a few years or months. No matter how long I have known them, I am so grateful for their friendship. They have helped me grow, they've inspired me, challenged me, and formed me into who I am today.

My friends are truly amazing. I mean it when I say that they have set the bar extremely high for everyone else who enters my life. They are always no more than a text or a phone call away, and I love it. There are times when something is happening in my life, and all I need is to shoot them a quick text in between moments asking for prayers. They are on it.

My friends have shown me what I want my life to look like. It's a bit of a joke but also has a lot of truth to it.

80% of my friends are engaged, married, and have children.

15% of my friends are in serious relationships, enroute to getting engaged.

3% of my friends are dating trying to find 'the one'.

2% of my friends are single and not mingling.

I'm in that 2%.

Of the 95% of my friends that are engaged, married or even having children (yes, I count fur babies too), or in serious relationships and will be getting engaged soon, they have really shown me what it is like to date and marry their perfect other half.

I've seen them go through fights with their significant others as well as encourage one another to chase after their dreams, even if it means that they won't be together any more. I've seen them choose the other person over choosing that they want, all because they love them.

I've seen them date in healthy and not so healthy ways.

I've seen us all make mistakes.

I've also seen us all recover and learn from them.

I'm not one to say I'm interested in dating. If a cute guy comes along, and we click really well, then chances are I'll be interested in you, but I'm not going to chase after every guy I see. And many of my friends are like this too.

They've helped me realize what having a healthy relationship can look like, how it can grow and prosper.

I'm forever thankful to them for showing me this.

Really and truly, whoever that guy is for me, my friends have set the bar very high on how to care for me and be there for me in all sorts of situations.

Just as I have seen my friends in some of their worst moments, they have seen me in all of mine.

During my sophomore year of college, I was going through a rough spot. I had just gotten back from my internship in Washington, DC and was back at school but didn't really have a student mentality. I had learned (a bit about) what the 'real world' was like, and I didn't want to go back to the 'school world'. During this time, a friend and I had *a few words,* to put it kindly. Now I can say that we are friends, but back then, we were trying and failing miserably.

She and I are just extremely different. I was an extrovert and chased things, while she was a major introvert who didn't.

I know it can seem trivial, but in reality when your whole world is your school's campus, a small bump in a friendship, let alone someone you see often, can call for a major breakdown in your friend's room.

I sat there crying on my best friend, Kierstin's, bed telling her all that was going on. I didn't know what to do about my friend, how to help her, how to get her to get out of her room. I didn't know what to say, or how to act or really just what to do. I was confused about being back at school and wanted to find a way to get back out into the real world and quickly.

She sat there with me, brought me tissues so I could blow my nose like a foghorn. When her roommate came and wanted to pop in, she asked her if she could do it quickly so we could keep talking, and I could keep crying in privacy.

She sat there on her bed with me while I cried and tried to figure out my life and my friend's. She said these very words to me, which have been monumental, "Gwen, you can't live someone else's life for them. We each have to choose our own." I realized right there that I wanted more for my friend, I wanted her to live a life like how I was living mine, chasing after each opportunity that came my way. She didn't, she wouldn't, she wasn't made that way.

Kierstin has been in my life for more than a decade, she's more than a friend, she's a sister. I love her with all my heart, and she cares for me through it all. She is one of my wisest friends, and enjoys a laugh like no other. She helps me make sense of all the crazy decisions I make, and she's there to give me a tissue or even drive around in search of a cup of water after ice cream, whenever I need one.

My friend Rachel, whom I only roomed with for a semester during our junior year of college, was destiny, or Jesus, whichever you prefer. We hit it off as roommates and have been best friends ever since. During my junior year of college, I was making some major decisions in my life, one of which would take me away from school and away from home.

Like I said earlier, this was the semester where I was in the middle of making a monumental decision about taking time off school to pursue missions or to continue my education at the time.

I let my thoughts and feelings on all these decisions go to the side as I celebrated my 21st birthday and continued to move into my dorm, help with a retreat, and then begin my first week of classes. On the very first day of class, I was off to my Cell Biology course, one that I was less than thrilled to go to. The entirety of the hour, my professor was handing us paper after paper, some we needed to sign, many were homework for the following day, some we needed as reference.

I was overwhelmed by all that was expected of the course and could only think about getting myself out of the room. It took all my willpower to stay in my seat, body clenched until she dismissed us. Whereupon I went straight to my car and drove to my mom's work, crying the entire way.

I wanted to leave school and do mission work.

During this whole crazy season of my life, where I was up late working on assignments, fundraising ideas, worship nights, being an auntie and friend, my roommate was amazing. She was there when I was sitting and crying on the floor of our room not sure what I had gotten myself into.

She was there when I didn't know why I was doing this, but I was, and she was there to support me.

She was there going on adventures with me (rooftops are a really good place to think).

She was there when I just needed a cup of coffee and a friend.

She was there when I wanted to make a fundraising video and yet had no idea how to.

She was there when we both couldn't sleep and came up with some genius ideas in the middle of the night. (Umm hello, a whole body dryer in each building to use when it snowed out, and we were cold, and it ran on swipes of our student ID cards! We are going to be millionaires).

She reached out while I was on the World Race to check in with me, weekly if not daily, to see how I was doing. She told me news in her life that helped me know I still had a place back in Indiana to return to.

When I came home and started going back to school, she helped me transition back home. She was my fairy godmother in helping me get my internship with Thirst Project.

Rachel, you are one of my best friends, a sister too. I couldn't imagine my life without you.

My friend Kellen and I have only known each other for about a year. We met doing an internship; leading up to it we would chat a few times a month. When we met in person, we hit it off immediately. He is awesome. He's one of those people that when you meet, you just know you're going to be friends for life. The way some of my friends put it, we just belonged in each other's lives.

He's amazing. He's a thoughtful guy, one who thrives on adrenaline and adventure, and one who encourages you to seek out the most in life. My kind of friend. While we were living together in January (all the interns lived together), I was telling everyone stories about my friends because I had received some amazing news about Rachel and her husband getting approved on buying a home! I was over the moon for them. Somehow while we were chatting about Rachel, I mentioned I had pictures and asked if I could show him. He obliged.

We sat there in the living room, going through the photos of my friends and family that I brought with me. I told the stories of how I knew each person and what their role was in my life. He listened to every story. He asked questions. It was just what I needed that day.

That month Girl Scout cookies went on sale. For a week, Kierstin and I were talking back and forth about how much we *loved* those cookies, and how we were trying to find them. One day on our way home, I saw a sign for Girl Scout cookies that were on sale. We followed the sign and I hopped out and bought three boxes of Samoas for us all to share.

I will always remember that week, when we truly became friends. We knew each other beforehand, but that was when we actually were friends in my book.

These are just three friends whose small acts of friendship that have impacted my life I wanted to share, but there are hundreds of thousands of more stories on my life-changing friends. Truly if you want to hear them, block out years of your life, and I will talk your ear off.

My friends know how to be a friend. I once heard this story of how a good friendship is like a two lane street. You each get to go your own way without taking over the other's lane. A bad friendship is a one-lane street. One where you each take turns or one just continues without regard to the other.

While my friendships have definitely had their one-way street moments, they are almost always a two-lane road. It is an honor to call my friends not just friends but family. They are amazing to me, and I only hope that I am half as amazing back to them.

While my friends and I have not always had amazing highs in our lives together, there are often times where our humanness comes out, and we fight, but I still live by an open-door policy. Literally and figuratively, I always keep my door open, and this is what I tell my friends. If we grow apart due to life, jobs, boyfriends, girlfriends, family, anything; my door is always open. I don't close it.

I forgive and let the past mold my future. I don't hold grudges. I respect decisions that are made.

But my door is always open.

It's open for you too.

Chapter Eight
World Race

When I was 21, I did the scariest thing I ever thought possible. I decided I was going to take a year off from school and do mission work. More accurately, God decided for me. Here's what happened:

My sophomore year of college, I started doing an internship in Washington, DC. It was an amazing semester of growth, meeting new people, and truly learning what I may want to do at some point in my life. While I was in DC, I had the honor of going to one of the best churches I've ever been to, National Community Church (NCC). While I was there, I realized just how much I wanted to help the world. NCC was strongly involved in mission work not only locally, but also globally. I tried my hardest to see if I could go on trips the semester I was there, or even fly back out for spring trips, but I couldn't make it work with my studies.

When I made it home and started back at school in January, I thought that the faster I push through school, the faster I could make it onto the mission field. I started planning on taking summer courses, maybe even winter term classes, just to ensure that I could graduate in May of 2016.

As summer rolled around, I was working on campus and taking both a summer accelerated Chemistry course and an online Statistics class. I thought life was fine. I was going to graduate in a few years, and I would be in the field. I didn't know what titrating an acid into a base mattered, how would it help me in helping others. (Due to this mentality, my chemistry professor and I were not the best of friends to say the least). haha

As my friend Rachel and I moved into our new dorm to start the fall semester, I was praying and saw something that would forever change my life.

It was graduation in May of 2016. I was walking across the stage, shaking hands with trustees, receiving my diploma, hugging my university president, smiling; excited for what was to come. But in my heart it wasn't right. I wasn't where I was supposed to be.

My view changed at that point. I was standing in the stadium, cheering on my beloved friends as they walked across the stage and received their diplomas. I wasn't graduating, but in my soul, I knew I was where I needed to be.

When I first started to pray about what I had seen, I thought it meant that I was no longer going to graduate college; that something would happen, or I would start something that wouldn't allow me to graduate (plot twist, it didn't!).

A little while later I heard a simple phrase from the Lord:

You won't be in America come January.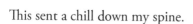

This sent a chill down my spine.

What am I going to be doing? Am I going to come back to school? Is this my next step? Will I learn what I'm supposed to do? Where am I going? Is this long term? Is this just for now?

My mind swirled with questions and very few answers.

During this crazy season of my life I was also taking a course, outside of my university, on missions called Perspectives. One of my friend's parents were the ones heading it up, which is how I learned about it. It was a fascinating course, learning about the 10/40 window, (the 10/40 window refers to the latitude and longitude of the area that is the most unreached of the world) and how to not just helicopter in but actually work to understand the cultures of these areas. It opened my eyes to the ways of the world. While I was taking this course, I talked with my friend's parents about the vision I had while praying, and what I had heard God say to me. They understood completely. They even told me about a program that I might want to look into called The World Race. It was an 11-month mission trip to 11 different countries, where I would work to help spread the Good News and be extra hands and feet for organizations.

After having heard from them what the program was like, needless to say, I was intrigued. I was looking at a few other organizations as well, some only a few months long, some six months, some a year or more. I applied to two different programs: one six months long, one 11 months long.

I applied to both the same week.

I got accepted into both the same week.

They both had to know my response the same week.

I realized that God really did want me to take some time off school and do mission work, otherwise, I would have gotten "noes".

Through a long week of praying and seeking which direction I was to go in, I realized it was the World Race, an 11-month mission trip to 11 different countries, so I accepted their offer while declining the other organization. I had complete peace over this move.

In just a few weeks after deciding to go, I was at training camp. A few months later, I was finishing my first semester of my junior year of college. A few weeks later, I was launching out to my first country, the first country I had *ever* traveled to, and embarking on an 11-month journey that would forever change my life.

Chapter Nine

Community

Do you remember summers as a kid? I *loved* summer vacations. My friends and I would spend *hours* together every single day. To the point where our parents would intentionally not let us hang out for a day so we wouldn't get sick of each other. Some of my best friendships and memories have come from those summers of spending hours together. We just got to *know* each other, like a deep knowledge of one another. We laughed, we told stories, we adventured. It was true friendship.

That was what it was like on the World Race. I met some amazing people on all of my teams, many of whom I still keep in touch with today. We got to know one another on a deep, spiritual level, not just surface level. We spent our days together and little time apart. It was like summer vacation for 11 months, except not all fun and games, but the weather was summer-like year round, which was a major perk.

On the Race, you're placed in a lot of high-pressure situations, which show your teammates your true colors very quickly.

My first month, my team and I were placed on our own in the city of Santiago in the Dominican Republic. It was probably the best first month a team could have. We all worked together, some of us getting up early to make breakfast, helping make dinner, family time around the table; we really just became a family. We knew how to use one another's strengths to best suit us as a whole. A week or so after we started working in the city, the home we were staying in got robbed. We came home from an off day of half of us exploring the city, and half of us going to the beach. When the group that explored the city made it back home, we were joking about dreams and how some of us had had some interesting ones the past few days. When we walked in the doors, I felt something odd, but was in a rush to get my journal to show my teammate some of my dreams. I walked back into the kitchen, and I knew something wasn't right. One of my teammates was already there, and two others came in after looking in their room and finding others' belongings strewn about. We realized we'd been robbed.

I raced into my room to see what was taken, I had my phone on me all day. but someone took my iPod, tablet, and headphones. Luckily nothing else, but my music was gone.

I broke.

I fell to my knees holding my beloved stuffed animal Daisy, crying. One of my teammates Sarah came and wrapped her arms around my shoulders and got me up onto my feet and helped me into the kitchen. She got me a cup of water and sat with me while I cried until I had no more tears left.

Part of my tears were for my material possessions I'd lost.

Part of my tears were for the violation of someone taking my things.

Part of my tears were for my music, a wonderful release for me and a way of connecting with God.

Part of my tears were wondering what the hell I was doing on the World Race if I was crying over losing my things.

As the week went on, God showed me I didn't need my music to connect with him. I found other ways.

The day after our house was robbed, we decided to take turns staying at home. The first shift was mine and a teammate's. We had lots of dishes to do and clothes to wash, so we set to work, both of us doing different tasks to keep the house tidy. I was standing at the sink washing dishes and started to hum some of the same songs that I had been listening to just the day before. Before long I was worshipping right there in the middle of the kitchen, just my voice, while washing dishes, nothing else. I didn't need my iPod to listen to music and grow closer to the Lord, I could just sing on my own.

A few months later, we were in the beautiful city of The Valley of the Angeles in Honduras having a debrief. Debriefs were a time set aside for us to come together as a squad to refresh ourselves mentally, spiritually, emotionally. Each day seemed wonderful. I was able to catch up with my friends from other teams, and hear how their months went. One day I woke up early to have a breakfast one-on-one with one of my squad mates. She has a beautiful soul, and I was excited to catch up on what her month was like. After breakfast, my stomach started to hurt some, and I got really bad diarrhea.

I went to see an old teammate who was a nurse about my situation for some medicine and a suggestion on what to do. "Hydrate and eat toast or dry crackers," she said, and I did so. Until a few hours later, and a fever kicked in, and I started bringing up all that was in my stomach and then some.

It was evening when the worst of it started to happen, and everyone else was worshipping and listening to a message. I ran into the bathroom and proceeded to relieve myself of everything that was inside. As I was busy, one of my squad mates, Kerry, came into my room calling my name. She came into the bathroom and found me sobbing into the toilet, delirious from my fever, unsure of what was going on. She stayed for a few moments, rubbing my back, praying over me, singing to me, and then went to get some nurses. A few nurses came back, and they tried to ask me what was wrong, I could barely get the words out. Sarah, the same one who helped me off the ground in the DR, came and sat on the bathroom floor with me, worshipping, rubbing my back, helping me drink water and Gatorade, and then rubbing my back once more as I brought it back up again. Sarah prayed over me. She didn't laugh when I fell asleep on the cushioned toilet seat only to wake up a few minutes later to continue. She helped me into bed when it had all mostly stopped.

I don't know what I would have done without those sweet friends taking care of me. Before the World Race, I prided myself as an independent person, one who could take of herself. Obviously, that wasn't the case, and I am so happy that I learned how to rely on others' strengths when I am weak.

On the Race, my teammates and I were together literally 24/7. There were times when we would be sharing a room and bathroom with 15 or more other girls. There would be one in the shower, one using the toilet, one using the mirror, and one using the sink. There would be times when we would barely have more than two inches in between us sleeping or on a bus.

Needless to say, we all got close quickly. As quickly as we grew closer with one another, our facades shed even faster. There was a deep-rooted authenticity that we all broke down towards to become our true selves.

There are a lot of aspects about the World Race that I love. We have this alumni page where anyone who has ever done the World Race and has a Facebook page can get on and ask for prayer requests, help with lodging, suggestions on what to do in various places, anything. It's a wonderful community that is created. I've met Racers that I wasn't on the field with, and we connected deeply simply because we have all been *there*.

There are quite a few people on my squad that I still talk to today. There's a deep connection that is created when you live life with people 24/7 for an entire year. It's a connection that doesn't go away just when you go home and no longer see one another. It's one that allows you to message each other when you're thousands of miles away just to see how their day is, chat for hours about work, friends, family, that cute guy we saw at work. It's perfect; it's family.

While on the World Race, it was *not* all rainbows and butterflies. It was hard. There were times I wanted to quit.

Like one day when we were in Botswana coming home from a safari. I had just broken my ankle a week or so beforehand and was still struggling. I didn't like not being able to do things on my own, and I was taking it out on my team. After a day of exploring, having one of the most amazing adventures I had been able to have that year, our drive home was a bit complicated. We couldn't fully remember how to get back home. We recognized some of the streets, but it seemed like we were going in a big loop. We were all calling out suggestions on how to get home: "Turn here." "No, go straight then turn right." "No, make a U-turn and go back then turn left." "No, at the light turn left and then turn right." My teammate was driving, and was relying on us to work together to get us home.

Something that I have always struggled with is the power of my voice. Growing up, I was a really shy girl. I didn't always say much, but I saw a lot. When I did speak up, oftentimes it felt like no one was listening. So that day in October when we were driving around in circles, and I was trying to get my suggestion across on how to get home, it *felt* like no one was listening to me. Although that wasn't totally the case. There was a moment where I was sitting in the backseat, I decided to say how I thought we got home, I said so, and someone spoke over me. There was the roar of cars all around us, the light had just turned green,a and we had to make a decision. My teammate driving decided one thing while everyone else said something different. Right there, I heard something in my head, *"No one listens to you."* It wasn't the truth, but I gave it power. This thought took advantage of my deep-rooted pain in feeling as though I didn't have a voice and took me down a deep spiral. I raised my voice to my teammates in the car and said something along the lines of, "Will you just trust me?" or "Will you just listen to me?" and the tone shifted in the car. This was more than just getting us home.

When we came home, my teammates gave me some hard feedback. The kind that cuts deep into your heart and makes you wonder what the hell you're doing with your life and where your truth is. One of my teammates said it was time to stop, it wouldn't be fixed in that exact moment, and I needed to process through it all. I went into the room we were staying, sat in the closet, and cried. I just wanted to hide from it all. One of my best friends came in and just hugged me. Moni said, "Oh Gwendy, I'm not here as your teammate, I'm here as your friend," and just hugged me and handed me tissues as I cried and tried to figure out what was going on.

Oddly enough, I did figure it out. I realized the long, deep pain I have in feeling as though people don't listen to me is that my voice isn't heard. I talked with my team and those involved in what happened. If I hadn't had Moni, my teammate and best friend, to come in and hold my hand while I was crying, I honestly don't know if the result would have been as positive.

Moni is amazing. She is a Godly woman, loves adventure as much as the rest of us, and really set an example. She is incredible, and I'm so lucky to call her my friend.

There's something that happens when you meet a group of people that you're going to be spending a long amount of time with. Your barriers break down faster than they would normally. You become authentic pretty quickly.

That's what happened with my teammates on the World Race. We quickly all became a family. Helping one another when we needed it. Acting as a well-oiled machine when we had to get things done. Seeing where one person's strengths were and where another was weak. It worked perfectly. Now I could go on for hours on how we really worked as family. There's an age-old saying that says when you begin to treat your friends as family and family as friends, things change.

That's what happened, We were family first and then friends. We saw the good, the bad, the ugly, the hard, the wondrous, the miraculous, all together. It was wonderful to say the least.

These people that I lived with and more importantly did life with were amazing servants of the Lord. They inspired me every day; I wanted to be more like them in all that I was doing. It was definitely not always easy, but it was very much worth it.

In January of 2017, I was able to do a semester-long internship with an amazing youth water organization called Thirst Project. My team and I met one another over an email introduction and proceeded to have video calls every few weeks to get to know one another. When we finally met in person, it was like we were four best friends who finally got to see one another. It was wonderful.

We lived in this incredibly tiny two bedroom, one bathroom apartment. For two guys and two girls, this was close quarters, and we got friendly quickly. Emily, my teammate, and I, shared a room. Kellen, one of the guys, had the other bedroom, and Sam slept in the living room on the couch. We were together almost every minute of every day while we were training in Los Angeles.

One Saturday after many changes had happened, I woke up at about 4 in the morning and got ready for the day. I needed to get out of the apartment and just think. I walked about a mile or so down the road to a local coffee shop only to find that they were closed. I waited around to see if they would open and decided to just go to the Starbucks on the corner. I sat there for hours, journaling, crying, drinking coffee and water, having to pee but not getting up. I cried, listened to music, and eventually realized that what is done is done and that I needed to move forward. When I got back to the apartment, my teammates were up and making pancakes and made some for me too. We all talked and cleared the air and were trying to decide what we wanted to do for the day. Around 3 o'clock in the afternoon we decided: *let's go to Joshua Tree to watch the sunset.* We all put on layers, grabbed our bags and snacks, and set off. We drove over two hours and paid over $30 just to watch the sunset. It was exactly what we all needed after the crazy week of changes.

Chapter Ten
Grandparents

2017 has been rough, it seems like I just can't catch a break from it all. It seemed like everything was going wrong. I didn't get my dream job, I had no money, was unemployed, and I moved back home. And then, as if matters couldn't get any worse, almost four months exactly to the day is how quickly I lost both my grandparents.

I won't forget how it happened. I couldn't forget how it happened.

The 21st of May 2017.

A few short weeks earlier, I called you, Grandpa. I was going to be passing through Asheville, North Carolina and wanted to stop by to see you and Granny. It took *guts* for me to make that phone call. I was in tears for a few days afterwards when you said that you didn't want to see me. It hurt. It really did.

A few weeks later I was home again. It was a Sunday, a Sunday like any other. Mom and Dad came home from church a bit after I woke up. Mom was falling asleep on the couch, and dad had already gone upstairs. Out of some odd feeling, I checked Mom's phone before I headed upstairs to write. Uncle Chris had texted her asking her to call him as soon as possible. I knew it.

I gave the phone to Mom and went upstairs anyway, giving her privacy.

As luck would have it, the internet wasn't working, so I came back downstairs a little while later and stayed downstairs to hear the news.

The doctors didn't think you would make it through the night.

Was I shocked? Yeah, Grandpa I was. I was sad too. I never actually got to say goodbye. The last thing I said to you on the phone was that I loved you. You said, *"Why? You don't know me?"*

But I do, Grandpa, I do. I know you from stories and pictures. I know I have a lot of questions. Like why were you the way you were?

I don't know if I'll ever know the answers, and that's hard, Grandpa, that really is. I want to know. I want to know why you chose to live out your final years in bitterness rather than awe of what you had done.

A lot of times people ask me how I came to be the way I am, what drives me to do so much. Do you want to know something, Grandpa? You have a lot to do with it.

When things started going south between you and Mom, I didn't know what to think of you and Granny. I loved you guys, you were family, but you weren't in my life. That was hard. My friends talked of their grandparents after every holiday, and I usually just got a card. I heard stories of the times you guys would travel and see the world and how much Granny loved to do things like that. You were the writer, which you passed on to me.

But you were also the world's biggest critic.

You see, Grandpa, I'm sorry we'll never be able to sit down and have a cup of tea and talk about life. I really am. It breaks my heart, if I'm being fully honest. I'm sorry you didn't get to see me graduate high school or college, and now you'll never get to see me write for a major publication, get married, or heck, even move out. I'm sorry you'll never read these words that I write as the tears fall down my cheeks.

I'm sorry you'll never get to know me. Just like I never really got to know you.

You left us with more questions than answers. You were always a closed book. Never opening more than the page you were currently on.

So here I am Grandpa, 23, sitting up in my bed well past midnight trying to sort through all of this. I don't know what is going to come of it, but I know one thing for sure.

As you and Granny grew older, you grew more bitter toward what life handed you and what you decided to do. Me, I don't want that to be. I want to be one of those people who when I get to be old, I can look back and smile at all the things I did. The crazy, the stupid, the courageous, the wonderful.

I did it, and I did it all.

I'm sorry you'll never get to see it. You chose your life, and thank you for doing so. You were a wonderful man, and you taught me a very valuable lesson to the day you took your last breath, for which I will be forever grateful.

We do miss you, and always will.

John M. Bergman, an author and father, who maybe wished he wrote a different kind of life.

Saturday September 23, 2017

My parents were planning on going to a wedding of a cousin a little ways away, and I had to work so I got out of going. Throughout the morning at work, I would get a message from my mom telling me what she and my dad were up to. I was trying to convince her to stay home so we could work on painting, but my dad sweet-talked her into going.

During the middle of my shift, I was overwhelmed with exhaustion. Sure, it was right after a big rush, and I hadn't had a break yet, but still it felt different. It felt like weariness to the bone. I asked if I could take my break sometime soon. As I got off the floor, coffee in hand, I went outside. I didn't want to get on social media and see what was going on, so I just sat for a while, drinking my coffee.

When I got home, bringing drinks to revive my parents from their drive, I knew something wasn't right. I was happy, it was a beautiful, sunny, Saturday morning, and I still had the rest of the day ahead of me. Then I saw my mom's face. Broken. Sad. Tear-stained. I just knew, Granny was gone.

I cried.

I cried tears I didn't know I had.

I cried until my eyes were sore from wiping them.

I cried until my nose was sore from blowing it.

I broke down in the shower after working outside.

Crying out to God, asking, yelling, "Why? Why now? Why Today? Why them? Why couldn't I know them? What happened? Was it my fault? Was there something I could have done? Why didn't they want to know me? Why, Lord?" I wanted someone to come and be with me, and yet I wanted to be alone from everyone.

Kierstin texted me asking me how I was, and I was so honest: I was spent. I was tired of crying, and I didn't know what else to do.

Not ten minutes later did she show up at my doorsteps, tissues, wine, and chocolates in hand.

We talked well past midnight. She hugged me while I cried. She let me tell stories, some of only parts that I remember.

I remember sitting on the kitchen counter, one of the few times they came up north to visit, Granny teaching me how to make meatballs. I couldn't tell you what was in them, but I knew they were delicious. We used the big mixer. We used the counter to shape them, and we baked them. We got so dirty, and I remember I was in a dress I had to change out of before dinner.

We laughed.

Another day, I remember that we all played Uno for hours. I couldn't believe all the adults sat there with us for so long playing. But they did, and I bet they had fun too.

I remember when we went down to visit them; I was older, maybe in middle school. The fashion then was to wear a cute embroidered camisole under a jacket, zipped up halfway. We 'dressed' for dinner, and that was what I wore, along with a pair of jeans. When we walked into their house, my Granny marched up to me, a slight smile on her face, and zipped up my jacket all the way, parted my hair over my shoulders and then patted them, smiled, and walked back into the kitchen.

That was who she was: a loving, caring, extremely old-fashioned, yet incredibly ahead of her time when it came to clothing and jewelry. She was amazing.

Granny,

I miss you more than words could ever describe. I miss the way that you cared for us all. The way that you chose the smallest of water pitchers to bring to the table for all of us when Aunt Ruth made her eye-watering, spicy enchiladas. I miss the way that you always wore the brightest colors. The way that you just wanted to make sure that your husband and family were happy. How without fail, every year I would get a card from you on my birthday, Valentine's Day, Christmas, and Easter.

Granny, I love you. I always will. I deeply wish, so much that my heart hurts sometimes, that you could have known who I am today. I wish both you and Grandpa could have.

You helped shape me. Mom says I'm so much like you, and I know that's the highest of compliments. You were a saint to her, and an inspiration to me.

I wish things had turned out differently. And if I'm being fully honest, I wish I never came to see you in the nursing home because you were no longer my Granny. You were just some old woman in a shell. It hurt to see you like that, so feeble, so unable to be the you who was so vibrant.

I miss you. I miss Grandpa. I hope that while you two are dancing together in Heaven, you look down every once in awhile to see what we're all up to down here. I hope you smile when you see us painting. I hope you smile and laugh when you see how much of a father Noah is to his little girls. I hope you remember all those hours we spent playing Uno when I break out the cards to pass the time. I hope you and Grandpa laugh whenever we all eat Mexican food.

I hope you both are proud of who your children, grandchildren, and great-grandchildren have become. We wouldn't be here without you; I just wish that you were more a part of our stories.

Marilyn Bergman, an amazing woman whom I share an original name with, a mother, an artist, a woman ahead of her time. We love you and miss you dearly. May you always be a part of our hearts.

Chapter Eleven
At First Sight

Are you a *How I Met Your Mother* Fan? If not, I will patiently wait while you go binge-watch all 9 seasons of it.

I'm waiting.

You had to know this was coming.

OK, seriously though it's worth it.

I don't want to spoil it for you, OK?

Fine, fine, if you insist.

It's one of my favorite shows, probably because it speaks to the hopeless romantic in me, but really it's just hilarious.

The very first episode Ted (the main character) falls in love, at first sight, with a woman he sees from across the bar. Say what?! Now until I was 18, I had never felt what Love at First Sight was really like, until I met my first niece at the hospital.

I was head over heels in love with her. There was a pulling on my heart strings when I laid eyes on her. I just *knew* deep down that I would do anything for her. From her precious little toes, to her button nose.. She was my everything.

When I started to travel, I fell in love with the kids I met along the way.

When I was in Honduras, I met the most amazing young girl, Tiffany[1]. Tiffany had been molested and abused growing up, and by the time she had made it to the children's home I was working at that month, though

---

1 For the sake of her and the other children in this story, their names have been changed.

she was about 15 years of age, her mental wellness was not a day over 5 years old. She was beautiful. Her heart was pure gold, and she just loved to laugh, smile, dance, and run. She was simply a child and an amazing one at that.

When we left her to go to our next location, my heart ached to say goodbye. I couldn't believe that I was leaving her and didn't know if I was going to make it back.

I met many young children during my travels. Some who wrote me letters to hold onto, some I have pictures with and look back upon fondly of our times together.

One teenager I met in the Philippines, Cindy*, calls me her aunt to this day. She is amazingly sweet and dreams of seeing the world. I know she will someday. I wouldn't be surprised if she becomes a diplomat, or even a doctor or a lawyer. She dreams of doing everything, and I couldn't be more proud.

I met one little girl, Sally*, who was the most precious baby I had the opportunity to hold that year. Now I'm not really a baby person. I loved my nieces when they were young, but I love them a lot more now that they can stand on their own two feet. As I was holding Sally the first day I met her, I was overcome with a love for her. How her parents could leave her in a park when she was just days old, I have no idea. It made my heart ache, but I am so happy that she was placed in safe, loving hands.

Something I have learned while I have met all these young children around the world is that they just want to be loved. And don't we all?

Don't we all just want someone to hold us, whisper in our ears how amazing and beautiful we are? How much we can change the world? How we can do anything that we want to do?

Jesus does that.

Jesus whispers into each of our ears just how special we are. He molded each one of us to be who we are today. He cries every time we cry. He cares for each little hair on our heads.

He wants us to have the best lives that we can. He *loves* us.

While I met each of these children: Tiffany, Cindy, and Sally and more, I felt not only my heart swell for them with Love, but God's love for them too.

I feel it with my nieces, with my friends, and with myself. He loves us so much, always has and always will.

Jesus lived an amazing life of Love. He did everything with Love as his mindset. Not fear, not worry, not success or achievement, but Love.

He loved in every situation he was in.

And that is how I try to live my life. I want to live a life of Love.

During my travels, it wasn't just people I met that stole my heart, it was cities:

Washington, DC, Los Angeles, San Francisco, Bristol, London, Portsmouth, Wales, Antigua, Guatemala, Port Elizabeth, Jeffreys Bay and Cape Town, South Africa.

They have all stolen my heart. My soul longs to one day return to each of these places and feel that love that I felt for the first time. That no matter how many miles away from my home I am, my heart feels so at peace there, because it feels as though I am traveling to another home. Almost like when you go home for a weekend from college and then go back to your dorm room. When I have been to each of these places, a stirring happens inside my soul. It is almost as though I am coming home or even not leaving my own.

Chapter Twelve
Yourself

Growing up I always wanted to look different than I did. My friends were either stronger than me, skinnier than me, their hair was straighter than mine, their eyes popped more, they didn't have zits. They were *better*.

Junior high was probably the worst. I think it is for everyone, honestly. I was going through puberty much like everyone else, and it was r-o-u-g-h. I hadn't yet gotten my growth spurt that would come in a few months, but I gained the weight that came with it, and I got a terrible haircut. I became the girl who woke up early in the morning to do my hair. I was so uncomfortable in my own skin that I turned inside rather than outside. As I got older and got into high school, my height skyrocketed, my weight leveled out, but I got really sick. With my sickness came skinniness, which at the time I loved, but also thought that I wasn't skinny enough. Every year a New Year's Resolution was to 'love my body,' but every year I never did. I always *tried*, I tried to get into shape, I tried to tone, and I even tried to tan to not be the palest in my friend group. This didn't really change until I got into my twenties.

It wasn't until I was 21 that I fully started to love my body. It wasn't just a switch to where I love my body every day and every second. It was still a struggle. There were times I got frustrated when pants didn't fit right, or when shirts didn't lie over my muffin. But something changed when I came home from the World Race.

When I came home, I *loved* what I had learned about myself while I was traveling. But coming home to a closet full of options, many of which didn't fit, was stressful in a way I never would have imagined. I hardly recognized the person in the mirror wearing my clothes. I felt gross. I felt fat.

We were warned when we were on the field that we would probably gain weight just because of stress, food, and life, but nothing could have prepared me for the weight I gained. Many of the clothes I brought with me no longer fit by the end. So when I got home, I was determined to try and get into shape. I started working out at school during my breaks from classes. But still, none of my clothes fit. So I did something that seemed crazy. I went and bought new clothes.

I went up a few sizes in jeans, and got some new, comfy oversized sweaters for the winter weather. Suddenly I didn't hate getting dressed in the morning. I didn't hate having to pull my jeans on and suck in my stomach just to button my pants. I didn't hate it when I couldn't just wear leggings to school or work. I didn't hate it because my clothes fit my body now. I realized that the clothes I had didn't fit my early twenty-year-old body, because I had bought the clothes when I was in my late teens.

I'm happy to have grown older, happy to have been able to go to college and gain the iconic Freshman 15 (or more). I was able to travel the world and eat some amazing food, and I saw some incredible sights. All in doing so, I gained some weight.

It has been a long journey to fully love my body. There are days when I don't fully love it, but it's all part of the process. A few months ago, I was realizing just how much I needed to continue to love my body, and I was reminded of the tale of a hag and model during my quiet time.

You meet a lady who looks like hag and a lady who looks like a model. You are instantly attracted to the woman who looks like a model. She's beautiful. She's breathtaking. You want to be her friend. The more you get to know her, to hang out with her, her beauty starts to fade. You start to hear her words, to see what they truly mean. Her words, they weren't beautiful. They were deadly. Her beauty faded, and you saw what was really inside. As you see what the model is truly like, not just her beauty but her thoughts and actions, you begin to think of the hag once more, "What is she like?" you wonder. And as fate would have it, your paths cross once more. You talk with her. You get to know her. You get to understand her heart, her hopes and dreams. Her words are breathtaking, inspiring, She's full of wisdom. Each word seemed to bring something new.

I was reminded that beauty is not just what we see as far as physical appearances. The most breathtaking beauty is what we find inside of ourselves. When we start to think kindly, speak carefully, love well, and humble ourselves; our thoughts, hearts and souls change from the bitter and become wholly beautiful. And that is what is reflected outwards.

As I've gotten older, I've been able to look at my friends in a different way. I see their strength, and I love that they have it. I see their body size, and realize just how beautiful inward and outward that they are. I love their hair, it's beautiful. Their clothing is wonderful and makes their eyes pop like they're under the sun. Their skin is as smooth as a baby's bottom. They are amazing.

It all started when I started changing the way I said things about myself. Instead of seeing my body and looking at it and thinking how gross, fat, ugly I was; I looked at my body and saw:

These pants look good today. My eyes are really bright. My hair looks amazing right now.

You want to know what happened? I changed the way I saw myself.

Chapter Thirteen
Don't Talk About My Friend That Way

Recently I heard this phrase on a podcast when two women were talking about body image. The host was telling a story of how she was trying on some clothes and mentioned how she hated the way she looked. Her friend who was with her, without missing a beat, responded with, "Don't talk about my friend that way." It struck a chord in my heart.

A few days later, I saw a meme posted with almost the exact same words on social media, with the tagline, "When you hear your friend talking negatively about themselves." And the person in the meme was shouting, "NO!"

Why do we do this? Why do we talk about ourselves poorly, but as soon as friend brings up their insecurities, we become the bouncer of their thoughts?

It didn't make sense to me, so I started to ponder that phrase, "Don't talk about my friend that way."

How would my thoughts change if I thought about myself the way that my friends do? Or if I found the beauty in myself that my friends see. It started to shift the perspective of my thoughts.

Whenever I lament to Kierstin about the rolls on my stomach or the size of my thighs, she sighs and says, "Gwen, you have like zero fat on your body. I don't even think your body can produce fat."

Of course that's a bit of a tall tale, but her heart is in the right spot. And just as she laments to me about her insecurities, I stop them in their tracks and tell her how beautiful she is, how much her body has gone through with her, how strong she is.

It's a cycle.

The other day I was getting dressed and pulled on one of my favorite pairs of jeans. The kind with the high waist, a bit of fading, but just worn enough to show how loved they are. They were a bit of a squeeze. I didn't even need a belt with them; I was still carrying some holiday weight. I glanced in the mirror and thought, "Yikes, we need to work out soon and get this under control." I pulled on a giant sweater to cover my stomach and hips and went about my day. I didn't want to think of my weight and where I was struggling.

As my day came to an end, and I was getting ready for bed, I saw myself in the mirror once more. As the unkind thoughts started to tumble in, I thought of a stronger thought, "Don't talk about my friend Gwen that way."

Sure, I could stand to lose a bit of the holiday weight I put on over Christmas. Sure, I could stand to tone up a bit more. Sure, I miss working out and running. But ultimately, I am beautiful and strong.

I don't say this to sound conceited, I say this to let you know you are too.

The next time that you look in the mirror and have body dystopia; you don't like what you see; you want to change; and the thoughts come barreling in like a crashing wave of how you aren't good enough, stop them. Don't talk about my friend that way. You are cherished, you are loved, you are beautiful, you are strong, you are worth it.

Chapter Fourteen
Self-care

Do you have social media? Have you scrolled through recently and seen at least one friend posting about taking care of themselves? Perhaps they called in late to work, took the day off as a personal day, didn't make plans in the evening. They were taking time for *themselves.*

Self-care is something that has always been talked about, but with added emphasis recently with the increase in knowledge of mental illness and increase in young people's suicide.

I, for one, am a huge advocate for self-care. I think of the motto: *If you can't take care of yourself, how can you take care of others?*

But I am also one who sucks at taking care of myself, at least until recently.

I have always been a doer, a go-getter, an if-I'm-not-out-and-about-and-moving-and-doing-then-I'm-bored kind of person. It wasn't until I came home from my internship in the spring of 2017 that I realized how badly I needed to take care of myself.

There were periods of time when I took care of myself during other parts of my life. At school, after my classes were done for the week, my roommate and I would both just climb into our beds and watch Netflix until or sometimes through dinner.

We would paint our nails, enjoy a hard cider while working on homework, go out to eat instead of eating in the cafeteria. It was small things but things that mattered.

On the World Race, my self-care routine looked a lot different. We didn't usually have WiFi, so I would paint my nails often, like once a week. I would read countless books, play tons of random card games, and sometimes, just nap.

In Washington, I explored every inch of the city I could. I spent time outdoors studying, reading, just relaxing under the sun and clouds. I would walk and not listen to music, but hear all the hustle and bustle of the city and the conversations of those around me. I would make delicious dinners. I ran almost every night.

Self-care is something most of us do without even realizing that we are doing it.

We sleep in once a week when we don't work. We just veg out on the couch and watch TV. We read our favorite book series over and over again. We treat ourselves to clothes, make up, movies, meals out.

We have a cheat day on our diets, where we can eat anything and don't feel bad about not exercising because we'll work it off the next day.

We have personal days stacked up at work to take a day just for ourselves every few months, a long weekend perhaps.

We know we need to, and sometimes we do, take care of ourselves, and sometimes we let it slip.

The conversation about self-care is so important. You're not neglecting other duties because you're taking care of yourself; you're setting yourself up for success because you're putting yourself first.

It's hard, believe me, to take care of yourself. Weeks will go by without me being able to paint my nails or sleep in.

I couldn't tell you the last time I had a day to myself where I just got to do everything I *wanted* to do over everything that *needed to get done.* Most of our days off consist of us making a to-do list of all the errands we have to run and chores we need to make sure get done so that our next week is a success. But what about *us?*

Sure, my laundry may be done and clean, the fridge stocked, and the house is vacuumed and dusted and the bathrooms are clean, but how am I *feeling?*

I'm tired because I just spent my day running errands. I'm tired because all I've done is chores. I've prepared for the week, but I'm tired in the anticipation of it.

I am tired of being tired, so I'm changing my routine.

When I have a day off, I don't start it with a to-do list. I start it with sleeping in, for as late as I can, or at least until my bladder makes it impossible to stay asleep.

I get up, have a few cups of coffee, eat a delicious breakfast, spend some time with God, and then I hit the ground running. Am I still tired? Sure, who's not nowadays, but I have a renewed sense of awakeness. I've taken care of myself first thing.

I can now run a few errands, but I'm going to come home and rest in the afternoon, read a book, watch a show, take a nap.

By the end of my day off, I'm still probably a little sleepy. I got stuff done, but more importantly I took care of myself.

The phrase is tried and true, you can't take care of others until you take care of yourself. Make time for yourself today.

Chapter Fifteen
Like Jesus

Do you remember that adorable children's song, *Jesus Loves Me?*

"Jesus Loves me this I know

For the Bible tells me so.

Little ones to Him belong

They are weak but He is Strong."

Remember now?

No matter how old I get, I will always remember this song. It's part of how I have learned to love so much.

As I have gotten older over the years, I have learned of all the different kinds of Love, many of which you just read stories about. But one thing that I am still working towards, and one that will never end, is learning to *love like Jesus*. It is something that I will never master because I am human and not God. But, it's something that I will always work towards.

You see, "because I am human" is a really easy excuse to get mad at a friend or a random stranger and not love them. It's easy for me to say (or think) when a friend is telling me a story *"Man, I don't like what you just said there, that's really rude."*

Or even…

"I asked you how you were ten minutes ago, and now we're talking about puppies and movies. How come you haven't asked me!?" And get mad and not want to love them.

But here's the thing about love: *It's a choice.*

Each day when I wake up, I have to make the conscious effort to love myself, to love my family, to love my friends, to love the random person who cuts me off in traffic.

You want to know why I do it?

 Because someone came before me and loved me at my worst moment. Someone came before me and knew every mistake I was going to make and still loves me. Someone came before me and knew that every time I got mad and said the F word and wanted to punch someone, key their car, throw coffee in their face; every dirty thought I have ever had; every middle finger I physically gave or mentally gave, someone still loves me.

God chose love in the form of His Son, Jesus, to come to Earth, to live among us, to dine with us, break bread with us, drink wine with us. To laugh with us over stories, to cry with us over losses, to help guide our ways.

He chose some*thing* in the form of one of us, a human, to come and make the ultimate sacrifice for all of us. Jesus went on the cross, endured ridicule, beatings, suffering, all for each one of us to let us know how much our Heavenly Father *loves us* and how much He wants us to love Him.

So each morning that I wake up, I choose to love. Some days, I do it a lot better than others. Some days when the sun is shining, people are nice, there's no traffic, and my hair looks and feels perfect, it's easy for me to love those around me. Some days when the clouds are dark, my clothes fit funny, I overslept, and people are mean, it's hard to love those around me, and I may not do a good job. But I know I can try again tomorrow, and I pray I get a tomorrow to redo today.

So choose love. Choose to love like God chose you so long ago when He sent His Son to us to show what true love really is.

Love can change you if you let it.

Chapter Sixteen

Don't Apologize for Wanting the Most Out of Your Life

A few days ago I was sitting at home and thinking about my life. If you can't already tell, I do this often. I was thinking about where I want to be in five years, and honestly I don't have a clue. I have no idea what I want to be doing jobwise, what I want my relationship status to be, or even where I want to be living. *But,* I know things I want to have done.

I started brainstorming.

I want to travel all over Europe.

I want to surf as much as I can.

I want to write, like really write.

I want to publish a book.

I want to go on a vacation with my parents.

I want to spend a weekend away with friends. Multiple sets of friends on multiple weekends.

I want to take a long weekend to Michigan and explore the cute little towns.

I want to create traditions like Thanksgiving dinner with family. Apple picking and making delicious food. Birthday celebrations.

I want to celebrate life.

I want to treat my parents more.

I want to learn a language and be able to speak it semi well.

I want to play guitar more.

I want to go to Canada.

I want to pay off my student loans.

The list just kept going.

My mom and I sat down to dinner one night, and I realized that I could achieve quite a few things on my list in doing just one thing.

"Hey Mom, I have an idea and a question."

"Yes sweetie, what is it?"

"Do you want to go to Europe with me? Or at least the UK?"

Her eyes sparkled. I get much of my wanderlust from my parents, but my mom specifically. She grew up in California and moved to Indiana during the Riots. When she and my dad got married, around ten years into their marriage they were talking: Europe or have kids. They tried to have kids while thinking about Europe, and lo and behold, that's when my brother came along. Kids won out. But she has always longed for going to see the beautiful country.

I realized that my version of travel is probably not something that my parents would be interested in or even able to do. Living out of a backpack, sleeping in hostels, living off of granola bars to save money, taking rides with strangers and staying in their homes, but the big kahuna was taking about six weeks off of work to actually backpack across Europe. So we settled on the UK, a two-week trek to see beautiful cities we have only read about or dreamed of seeing.

I was ecstatic! I was physically planning on going back to a country that has stolen my heart, and I couldn't be happier at the possibility. I told my mom that even if she can't go, I was still going to go, I want to go, I need to go simply for myself.

I texted a few of my friends after we started talking and tentatively planning and told them about it. Many were enthusiastic, some a bit skeptical, even my dad wondered why I wasn't using my money for something else. Which is when I was once again reminded that I *don't need to apologize for living the life that I want to live.*

We are not all made the same (Praise the Lord!). We all have different hopes and dreams. Sure, at some point, I will probably dream along with the rest of my friends of living somewhere consistently and having a steady paying job, but until then, my dream is to see the world and all who live in it.

I am by no means a needless spender. I don't simply throw money at things I don't use (ok, well sometimes, but we all need a little retail therapy every once in awhile). I plan, I save, I work hard, and I *love* to travel.

One of my friends asked me about bills, "Gwen, don't you have bills to pay? How can you travel and pay for plane tickets, and places to stay, and food, and everything else while you're there when you have bills?"

I am *always* going to have bills. My student loans will probably be paid once I've sold all the organs I can or until I die. It was my choice to go to a private university, and it paid off. I loved my time there. I will always have medical bills, from blood work to paying for when I was sick in high school, to the chiropractor I try and go to once or twice a month.

I will always have car insurance and a phone bill and food to buy and clothes to get.

But I won't always be 24, with nothing really tying me down except for my family and friends. I won't always have the flexibility I have with my current job and my ability to save money to travel. I won't always be able to just say, "Hey Mom, Dad, do you want to go to the UK for two weeks next spring or fall? If we book tickets by Thanksgiving they'll be the cheapest, and if we go in April, we'll be right before the big spring and summer rush. We could wait until fall, but I think spring might be more fun."

I am not a conventional type of person, and I don't pretend to be. I do what I love because I love it. I'm responsible with my time and my money. Doing something you love is worth the price.

All in all, if you're like me, if you have a thirst for travel and just want to see the world, work hard, and save money and do so. You don't have to explain your life to your friends or parents on how you use your money. It's your money.

You also don't need to apologize to anyone for choosing to live your life the way that you do. It is your life. There will *always* be people who ask me like my dear friend did, "Gwen what about bills?" or like my brother and dad and question how I am using my money and time.

It's my life, and I not only want to live it my way, but I want to be proud of what I did and take chances when I can. Not regret it later.

Chapter Seventeen
Love Your Singleness

When was the last time you logged into Facebook? I know, a throwback social media platform right? But one that truly changed the game for social media to come. Yes, I still use it. Yes, I have the app on my phone even. But that's beside the point.

Have you ever logged onto Facebook, perhaps multiple times a day, and been bombarded with your current friends, high school friends, that person who sat next to you in your math class in college, and work friends changing their status to "Engaged"?

Is it really just me?

Good, I didn't think so.

Just a few weeks ago one of my very best friends got engaged—finally. We've been waiting for it for a while and truly couldn't contain our excitement when the moment finally happened.

There's a funny thing that happens when your friends get engaged though, or even when they get married, have children, or buy a house. No matter the joy you feel inside for them and the new steps they are taking, you start to look at your own life and wonder what the heck you are doing. This happened to me once again when said friend got engaged. I looked at my life and thought: *what am I doing?*

I love weddings, I love marriage, I love love. But I am nowhere close to waiting to be married. Yes, I would love to be at some point, but not right now.

Right now I want to consume my life with the things that I love: family, friends, coffee, adventures, being the best auntie to my adorable nieces, being a good friend to my friends, investing in people and relationships and places that I want to go see.

Right now I want to focus on myself. I want to improve my health. I want to learn another language and more than just the phrases in Spanish and French that my Mom and I mix up while we are cooking. I want to be able to speak it!

Right now I want to learn more about who I am.

There's the adorable movie, *How To Be Single* that came out a few years ago on Valentine's Day. I honestly thought it was another one of those *Valentine* movies that wouldn't hold any ounce of truth, and therefore never went to see it in theaters. I ended up watching it on my flight back to the States last summer and *loved* it. Of course as I was telling a coworker about it recently, I prefaced the excellent movie with mentioning that I was probably oxygen-deficient and sleep-deprived, so I'm not sure how wonderful it actually was. (I just watched it again and it truly is wonderful).

If you ask anyone who is in a serious relationship, they say to cherish your single years. We shouldn't wish them away hoping that the next guy we swipe right on, the next guy we wait on, the next guy to buy you drinks will be *The One*. We should live our lives in anticipation for these things.

Are you who you want to be when you get married? Are you the type of person who wants to invite someone else into every little space of your life?

If you're like me, you're nowhere close. I'm not who I'm going to be when *The One* and I find each other (because yes, I do believe that we will grow one another, but I'm not yet there either).

Singleness isn't a curse, it's a blessing. We can live it the way that we wish.

I can pack up my bags tomorrow and move to England.

I can decide I want to speak Finnish and learn it.

I can cut off all of my hair.

I can go hike the Appalachian Trail, the Pacific Crest, I can do *anything*. I don't need to spend this time of *single*, of *waiting*, just sitting. I can spend this time *doing* and *loving* who I am, where I am, what I am.

Love your singleness, because one day it may be gone and you just might want it back, if only a small taste. ✦

Section Two

Vulnerability

I remember my first month on the World Race and one of my teammates told me that I reminded him of an onion. At first I was a little taken aback and thought, "Oh my goodness, how can I be an onion?! Sure they spice up food, but that's gross!"

He went on to explain that the more he got to know me, it was like he was peeling back layers to really see who I actually was. Once he explained it, I was actually flattered.

I never realized how many *layers* I truly had until that moment. I didn't always wear myself and all that I am on my sleeves. I showed who I was in moments, sure. But there wasn't this super easy synopsis that you can find on CliffNotes about who Gwen actually was.

There's a lot that's happened in my life that hardly anyone knows about. There's a lot that hundreds of people know about. There are some not amazing moments that only a few people have shared with me. There are some incredible moments that have gotten a ton of likes on Instagram. And there are some that I wouldn't imagine sharing with the public.

I've found that in my 20-some years of life, vulnerability is something that I equally struggle with and excel at. Vulnerability is this beautiful way to bridge the gap between how people view our lives on the outside to actually sharing with them what is going on.

It can be painful. It can be stressful. It can be scary.

I've learned how no one is perfect. I've learned that it's okay to be different. I've learned that things don't always happen the way that we once thought that they would.

But when we're able to look back and see all that we have learned through it, I think that *that* makes it worth it.

Chapter Eighteen
Perfection

While I was on the World Race in 2015, I was in my pressure cooker. I grew more in those 11 months than I have in some parts of my 20 some years of being alive.

One of the hardest things I had to learn was learning to love who I am and where I am in life. Growing up I struggled to be the *perfect* daughter. My brother did not make my life very easy. He chose a route and the way he wanted to live that left me feeling like I wanted to be the easy child and to not have Mom and Dad worry about me. It was hard, and I'll never forget when I realized just how hard it had been for me.

I wrote about it in a blog post during my time in Haiti, I would love to share it with you.

On our last morning in Haiti before we left for Costa Rica, Papa and I were spending the morning together with a beautiful sunrise and a cup of delicious coffee. He told me that I didn't have to be perfect or strive for perfection and performance. As I wrote these words down in my journal, I didn't know what they meant until Papa took me down memory lane.

I realized I set bars for myself that I felt like I had to reach. Even back in elementary school I wanted to outshine my brother and his grades, and it was that way as I got older too. My friends who were wonderful in school or had perfect attendance, I tried to reach that as well. It was all about getting the best and being the best in a way. I would place friends' accomplishments in front of me and work toward them and better, like how fast one can run a mile, a grade they got on a test or paper, making the Dean's list, likes on Instagram. Any and everything became comparison and I turned it into me trying to reach 'perfection'.

As I began to work through this before breakfast and on the start of our car ride, I asked God another question: "What am I supposed to write about this month?" He told me I already knew. I began to think about and realized this potential blog was terrifying to write. I was going to write about how I am broken, not perfect. 'Why?' I asked Papa, this seemed like something I would never write, never want people to see. And that is when it struck me.

You see, you, whomever you are reading this right now, I am about to tell you my life and be vulnerable with you. I didn't want to write this blog because it's not simply showing one side of the story; it's showing me in a vulnerable state. Not me on the mission field but a result of growing closer to my Father.

I am not perfect. I am broken. Jesus is the glue to recreate me.

I no longer have to strive to reach any bar that is set except for the one with the label Princess of the King of Kings. And that one, for that Crown, I am called to be myself, which I am going to begin to walk in more fully.

I am a daughter of the Most High, with scars on her heart from her past and cracks that need mending. I am beginning to be remolded and retaught who I am with a new bar set, which is none in this lifetime.

I'll admit this 'perfection' bar is hard to understand, realize, and wrap my head around. But I wasn't called on the Race because I had my whole life figured out. Much to the contrary, I was called to relearn who I am as a Daughter.

I don't have to be perfect, strive to reach any bars, or conform. I am me; the one He called me to be.

When I finally realized this about myself, I felt *free* in a way that words almost cannot express.

I'm not going to say that after this beautiful realization in Haiti that I have no longer struggled with being *perfect*. That would be a downright lie. I have and do struggle with it daily. Whenever I start a new project, I want to jump from being a beginner to knowing all that I can about it. I want to be the best; I don't want to have to *work* towards it.

Then I'm reminded that it's okay to be a beginner, in fact I should encourage it. For if I was never a beginner, I would *never* get to learn new things and that is so important when it comes to growing in life.

Chapter Nineteen
Grace

As you can tell, I struggle with perfectionism. When I want to do something, I want to do it right, the first time.

But that's not life. I find it really easy to give grace to people who are learning. Remember that one student in class who always asked questions? Sometimes they were anticipating what the professor would say, or they just need it repeated once more in order to get all the words to click, or maybe they blanked out for a few seconds and need to hear it again.

I totally understood that student because usually it was me. I *love* asking questions. I love learning more.

Just recently I got to the point at work where I just *know* how to do my job. I slip into my role with ease, no matter where I am placed. I just know what to do and how to do it. When new people get hired, it's a little rough. There was one day where a new coworker was having trouble ringing people up on the POS system. I hopped over and helped, hitting the buttons that needed to be pressed. It was easier. It got the job done quickly and the line kept moving.

But I didn't *teach* them where to find the buttons. After the patrons had left and the line slowed, I told them where the buttons were and was reminded of my first job, how I had absolutely no idea what I was doing.

So, I took a deep breath, and decided that I would help and *teach* rather than just *do* when someone was struggling.

We're all beginners at some point in our lives. If my parents had decided that when I started walking or speaking that it would have been easier for them to do it for me, I never would have learned, well *anything*. So next time it takes me a little while to get the hang of something new and someone actually takes the time to teach me it, I'll be extremely grateful. And, more importantly, the next time someone else is learning something, I'm going to give them some grace to take their time to learn it, and not rush them. Because we're all beginners at some point.

Chapter Twenty
Trust and Growth

While you are traveling, living, and sharing life with others, it gets hard. You see everyone at their highest and lowest moments, and they see yours. It's almost as though there are no closed doors, everyone can see everything. During many of these moments of transparency, I received some hard feedback from some beloved teammates.

It ended up being a reoccurring theme during my World Race: I have trust issues. In month 3, we were staying in the middle of the jungle in Costa Rica. One of my teammates and I were given the option to clean the house rather than go work in the fields and needless to say, we jumped on it. Our job was to clean the car, clean the kitchen, and sweep the entire house. Before everyone left, I asked my teammate if she would make sure that our host left us everything we needed, or at least show us where it was.

I asked her during breakfast, I asked her after breakfast, I asked her as we were all getting ready for the day, I asked her while we were sitting and waiting. Each time I asked her, I heard my voice saying the words, "Don't forget to ask." Even though my brain hadn't consciously processed it through.

Later that night during team time, I knew it was coming before she even said it. "Gwen, why didn't you trust me to ask about what we needed?" I did trust her, I really did. I just had a history of asking people to do things, and they never got done; I would have to pick up the slack.

The next day we sat together and had a heart-to-heart. I told her about my past of relying on others and being let down. I told her I heard myself ask her so many times the day before but hadn't consciously thought to ask her, because I knew I already had. I asked her to forgive my actions as they said I didn't trust her. She challenged me to forgive those who had let me down and to not hold what friends had done in the past with the way that our team operated together.

It seemed so minor, friends letting you down, but it had caused a deep root to grow in my heart and my thought processes. *If someone says they will do something, will they really, or will they just let me down, and I'll be stuck cleaning it up?* If it hadn't been for my teammate to call out my trust issues in love, it probably would have been years down the road when they came out in full force and caused me to really look inward and try and figure out what was going on.

A few months later, one of my dear best friends and teammates help me realize something else, my words don't always come out the way that I mean for them to. We were in Swaziland for the month, a beautiful, peaceful month. Our biggest concern was the lack of water that we had on base and our accessibility to it. While we were getting ready for the day, I was looking around for some water to refill my bottles and my teammate, Moni, asked me something along the lines of "Is there water for everyone on our team?" (We had to walk four miles to our ministry location and four miles back each day. We also needed water while we were there.) To be fully honest, I don't remember the exact words that were used, but I remember raising my voice and not speaking in love. We went about the rest of our morning, walked to our ministry site, and played with the kids.

After a hard day at ministry, we were walking four miles back to our campground where we were staying in Swaziland. My friend Moni and I had had a small argument that morning and it was lingering. We were both holding the hands of a small boy and walking and swinging the child when I looked over at her and said, *"Moni, can we talk?"*

Those words were powerful in opening a conversation that has helped me to be who I am today. We talked about it for four miles. *Why had I raised my voice? Why had I felt like I needed to get water over everyone else? Why did I worry there wasn't enough? Why had my tone come out the way it did?*

By now, this argument is so far into my past that I can't remember what exactly was said, how we forgave one another, or how we chose to move forward. What I do remember is how Moni, and so many other teammates, always told me the traits of my character that I needed to work on in love. They never once pointed a finger at me, rude, thoughtless, prideful or worse. They let the argume and then as I was sitting in the sorrow and shame of it with me at first while we wrapped our heads and hearts around w.. happened and then they helped me stand up and walk out of it; knowing I had identified what it was that caused me to speak out and trusting I would continue to work on it.

Daily it seemed on the Race I was reminded of just how much growing I needed to do to be more like Christ. With being back home, I have taken many of my hard times of growth and have used them as moments of reminding for myself and sharing with others. No matter how hard it gets during the growing seasons, I am always reminded that growth is not rainbows and butterflies. Even when our Instagram pages are full of inspirational quotes and double-tap-worthy photos with the captions of how much we have learned and how wonderful it is, sometimes it's really hard and just sucks.

But one of the most double-tap-worthy things I have learned about growth is:

Embracing the suck, embracing the fact that we don't know when it will get better but that it will, makes it a whole lot easier.

Chapter Twenty-One
Let's Get Real

There's something powerful that happens when you stop lying to yourself. I'm not talking the lie of: *"I'm going to workout every day this week,"* or the, *"Just one cookie,"* or even, *"One cup of coffee is enough for today."*

I'm talking about the: *I'm okay* lie.

One of the most magical sentences I have ever heard is: It's okay to not be okay.

I've learned that it's harder on my emotions, my physical body, my mental capacity to say I'm okay when I'm really just alright, or just hanging in there, or even sucky.

When I constantly tell myself I'm okay, when really inside I'm going crazy, I have a harder time convincing myself that everything is really and truly going to be okay.

There's this (in my opinion not super helpful) phrase that says: If you smile long enough, it'll actually be true. yea no.

I do believe in the power of positive thinking, but I also know how harmful it can be to not fully come to terms with what is going on inside.

In the late spring of 2017 I lost my Grandpa. Now, my grandparents and I unfortunately were not very close, but that's not the moral of this story. When my family and I found out about his passing, my mom and I packed a bag and drove to North Carolina to help figure out the house and all the other arrangements that had to be done.

I would never wish this on anyone, but when someone in your family passes that has a close relation (if only blood) you start to think about who is going to pass next. It's an unfortunate reality. With my Grandpa passing and my Granny not being too far behind him, I started to think about what will happen when my parents pass.

Will I be in Indiana? How will we get rid of all their stuff? What do I want from them? Who is going to go first?

With all the questions of an uncertain future lingering, I started questioning my own life:

What am I doing working as a part-time barista? Why don't I live on my own? Could I actually afford that? How am I going to pay off my student loans? If I have children will they be stuck paying them off? Do I really want to get married? Heck, do I really want to date? Why am I gaining weight?

And the big kahuna of a question:

What am I doing with my life?

During this whole transition period, I came home from an internship, got a job at a coffee shop, was in the second week of my training, third week of being home from my internship, and then my grandpa passed away. So I spent a week in North Carolina getting his items in order, came home, got thrown back into work, tried to hang out with friends, and tried to get back on track.

But I was just winded from it all.

When I came home from North Carolina, I said I was ok, that I was doing alright. But I wasn't.

I wasn't doing *okay,* I definitely wasn't anywhere close to *fine.* I was hurting, I was confused, I was processing what was going on while trying to figure out what was next.

When I *finally* came to terms with where I was and all the questions that were swirling through my mind, you want to know what was amazing? I could finally be real with my friends on what was going on.

I no longer said, "Yeah, it's going okay. Just trying to figure it out." I was able to say: "You know, it's hard right now. I know sometime it's going to get better, but right now really sucks. It has sucked for a few weeks right now. There are days that are really good and others that are really hard. I don't know what I'm doing or why I'm doing it, but I'm here, and it has to get better right?"

Spoiler alert: It does.

When you start to be real with yourself on what's going on in your life, you can finally be real with others too.

Chapter Twenty-Two
Dream Job

Remember when you were little and you dreamed of being a princess, president, a teacher or a lawyer?

Well I dreamed of being a famous singer. Surprise! I know I'm not one, but that was my dream growing up.

As I got older, my dream for my life started to change. I realized I didn't want to be just one *thing*, just one *job*. I wanted to do a myriad of things.

My second-to-last semester in college, I started to really think about what it was that I would want to do when I graduated. *Did I want to continue on in school? Was there a country I wanted to go to? Do I want to stay in Indiana? Do I want to stay in America? Do I want to work for the government? Do I want to work with non-profits? Do I want to go back out onto the field?*

These were the types of questions that swirled in my mind as I started my courses again in January 2016.

One of my courses that semester worked directly with nonprofits: *Writing and Editing for Nonprofits* was the official name. We were encouraged to find an organization that we could work with for the different projects we had. We could work exclusively with one or switch for each of the projects. I saw this as a perfect opportunity to find *the* organization for myself.

I made this incredibly long list of all the organizations I have dreamed of working with: Surfing for Change, Charity: Water, Thirst Project, Adventures in Mission, The Water Project, Changing Tides Foundation, SurfRider Foundation and many others. I started to research each of these organizations, and see which would be the best for me, one of which I actually got to hear about in person.

When I came home from the World Race, I started working at a local coffee shop just minutes from my house. One of my first shifts there, I met this really amazing guy. We bonded over our love for travel and love for coffee. Somehow during our conversation, he mentioned an organization called Thirst Project. He even mentioned how the CEO was his friend, and they were grabbing drinks together that night and invited me. Part of me wanted to go. The group sounded interesting, and I wanted to make new friends, but I declined since I wanted to spend time with my family and didn't really know the guy.

I pulled up Safari on my computer one day after class and started my search for the best organization with my handy pal, Google. I began my search with Thirst Project. As soon as I went to the website, I fell in love. The message: creating a socially conscious generation, bringing the power of youth to help END the global water crisis. I loved it all. I wanted to be a part of it. I looked for ways to get connected and involved and found this amazing internship that was twice a year: fall and spring semesters, where you would travel across North America speaking to middle schools, high schools, and colleges on the global water crisis. Educating students and helping them get involved and help change the world.

It was my *dream*.

From that moment on, I started working exclusively with Thirst Project for each of my projects for the class. I loved everything that I was able to do with them. I loved talking with the staff; they were so kind and friendly.

I was even able to meet the CEO that spring.

As summer came and passed, I was anxiously waiting to hear that applications were live for the internship in the spring of 2017. I checked the website weekly wanting to hear it was out. Early September I saw a Facebook post about the application being open and set to work. Many of my friends helped me create the most perfect resume to send. It showed everything about who I was as a person, not necessarily my job records but what I could do and loved to do.

They swiped right and I got an interview, and then a second interview. Then, at 4 AM on a Saturday morning after a restless night of no sleep wondering if I got the job or not, I rolled over and checked my email. There it was, my dream job was officially mine. Needless to say, I couldn't go back to sleep. That day was one of my favorites; nothing could take away my smile. I was so happy.

My internship really was amazing. It was an absolute dream come true. I *finally* got to see California, a state that had stolen my heart even though I had never been there. I met some incredible people who are insanely passionate about ending the global water crisis and helping empower the youth of this world to do so.

I got travel to more states than I had been to beforehand. I got to see America, all the little nooks and crannies, the mountains, the oceans, the small little one-stop spots. Let me tell you something, America is beautiful.

It wasn't an easy internship though. I set the bar high for myself, in hopes of getting a job with them afterwards. I fell asleep listening to my speech in hopes of memorizing it. I spent lunch breaks on the roof, saying the presentation and looking out over the city. I dreamed of what the road would be like.

When my teammate and I finally hit the road, it was a bit rocky. We thought differently and had different personalities.

One of the greatest life lessons I have learned is how to choose your battles. It's a hard line, trying to decide what is really worth your time in standing your ground. During our time on the road together, I had to choose *a lot* of battles, and I let many go too. While the World Race was my pressure cooker, this internship was hers. Just like on the Race, it wasn't always easy, and it certainly wasn't always pretty. There were days when we would be so frustrated with our situations, and yet there was nothing we could do.

We would get stuck in traffic for hours. We even missed a presentation because we underestimated San Francisco's traffic.

As our tour was coming to a close, so came one of the hardest weeks I have ever had to bear. We had a conference call with our other team and our home office. The final thing that was said was that the other team would be coming back for another tour in the fall. I felt my heart drop. I couldn't believe it. I stammered out a "Congratulations" and the call ended. My teammate turned and looked at me and asked if I wanted to talk about it. I gave a hard "No." I grabbed my phone and headphones and went outside. I had to get some air into my body as it felt like the world was falling all around me.

I called my mentor as tears rolled down my face and tried to explain what had happened. She knew the struggles I had been facing on the road and let me rant until my throat was raw from crying and speaking. She had to get off the phone for work but told me she was praying for me and God had some plan up His sleeve. I knew she was right but I needed to hear more.

I called Rachel and told her everything that had just happened. She was as dumbstruck as I was. She didn't understand any more than I did. She let me talk, she let me cry, she told me it's ok that it's not ok right now. She also told me: *Sometimes we don't always know the Why and sometimes we never will. We just need to know Who is in charge.* She tried to take my mind of off it all.

I felt like a bad friend to my other teammates. I wanted to be so happy for them but all I could focus on was how they got something I wanted so badly. *Could I still be happy for them even though my own heart was breaking?*

Yes.

I called my supervisor a day or two later and talked to her about the decision. I understood why they chose the other team, but I needed to hear more of the reasoning behind it. It wasn't easy to hear that they were the better team, but it did help to know.

The next day, as we were getting ready to leave for our next city, I got a text message from my boss back home. I had been working at a local coffee shop the year before I left, and it looked like I would be working there when I came home too.

I read her message while we were about to leave the house. Things had changed at the store, and I didn't have a job when I came home.

I was coming home in two weeks.

I drove us to our next presentation in tears. I was sobbing, yelling, telling my teammate how crappy this week had been. I didn't know what to do. I called my mom and told her and then I called my manager, I *needed* to know what was going on. Just like with my supervisor back in LA, I had to hear it from them.

She told me that things had changed within the company and she no longer had the jurisdiction to offer me my job back. I didn't get it, I was coming home in two weeks, and now I didn't have a job.

That presentation after the conversation with my manager was a blur. I remember I sat at the merchandise table while my teammate spoke. When we left to go to our next homestay, I was tired, I was trying not to cry anymore, but there were still tears left to be shed.

A few days later, the last day we were in North Carolina, I gave my second-to-last presentation. It was at a Paul Mitchell Beauty School. When I had woken up that morning, something was different in my spirit. Something had shifted.

In the final moments of my presentation was my call to action; I connect my whole story to one final point, the famous quote by Gandhi, "Be the change you wish to see in the world." Usually I talk about how I had gotten sick in high school, but that day, I knew I needed to talk about the fire that I was walking through right then and there. I stood there on the stage, feeling everyone's eyes on me, I started, "Here is where I usually talk about life growing up, but today, there's something different I want to say. Have you ever just gone through a rough week? Like no matter what happens, you just keep getting knocked down?" I raised my arm high in the air, and the students mumbled their agreement and some put their hands in the air too.

"So you know what I'm feeling. This past week I found out I didn't get not one job that I wanted but two. I was hardly considered for one and then a second, a job that I would have when I get home in *two weeks* was no longer available to me. You can ask Emily, (my teammate) but this week has been hell for me and I probably haven't been the best teammate.

"Every day when I would wake up, it felt like I was reliving it all. Each rejection. Each decision that I was trying to pinpoint as to *why* this was happening to me. And yet I was coming up short because I didn't know why. But I did know something. I knew that just like when I was younger, I could let my circumstances define me. I could let the fact that I didn't have a job in *two weeks* define who I was going to be for the rest of the time on the road and who I was going to be when I went home.

"Yesterday, I would have said I was that person, but today I woke up and decided that I didn't want to be that girl. I didn't want to be the girl who didn't know what was next, who was so worried about finding a job to pay off her student loans that she didn't cherish each moment she had on the road and each time she got to tell someone the dream that she was living right now. So I'm moving forward. I'm still working, I've still got two weeks left of this amazing internship, and I'm not giving up. I'm not that girl. I'm the girl who is taking the circumstances that are happening, but I'm still moving forward. I'm still working, I've still got two weeks left of this amazing internship, but I'm not giving up.

"So maybe you set some goals for yourself for this year, and come the end of January, you are so off track you don't know how to get back to them. Maybe you were in a bad relationship that's left you bruised. Maybe your home life wasn't amazing growing up, and you didn't have a lot of opportunities. Maybe life just hasn't been that great to you and you're tired of fighting.

"You can stand there each morning when you wake up and say, 'Yeah, life has been hard and sucky and stressful, and it still is and always will be.' Which is exactly where I was until this morning. Or you can stand there and say, 'Yeah, my circumstances have been hard and rough, but that's okay because I can change them. Each day is a new day, and I can decide what today is going to be.'

"Because friends, we have the power to change the world."

When I finally got home after my internship, I was a mess. I was tired from the lack of sleep the last four months, from the constant movement, and more importantly I was emotionally spent. The first weekend I was back, I applied for a job at Starbucks thinking it would be a good job in the interim until I found something else.

Almost four months later, and I'm still there.

I've done *a lot* of thinking these past few months. I thought about dreams I had growing up, when I was in college, and every time I have travelled.

I dreamed of being a famous singer when I was little.

I dreamed of writing for a surf magazine.

I dreamed of being an author.

I dreamed of running a hostel.

I dreamed of running a coffee shop.

I've had so many dreams and while some have come true, others are still waiting. Will they be next?

I really have no idea. I don't know how long I am going to be a barista at Starbucks. I don't know if I will ever write for a surf magazine. I don't know if I will ever live outside of the US for an extensive period of time. But I do know that even though this dream job of working with Thirst Project long term didn't come to pass, it doesn't mean I can't still be involved in helping end the global water crisis. It's a passion that is near to my heart, and I want to see everyone in the world have access to clean water.

Just because I'm not on their payroll doesn't mean that I won't still help change the world in some way.

So friend, I hope you know that if you don't get that job you are drooling after, you're not the only one. It's hard; it's really hard when things don't turn out the way you want them to.

It's hard when you're standing in the hallway hovering at a closed door. But friend, turn around, there are hundreds of other doors out there for you to choose from. Some are just an arm's length away, others you may have to walk to get there. But they are there.

Believe me.

Chapter Twenty-Three
Words

I fully believe that words hold more power than we give them.

When I was a freshman in college, a friend at the time said some quite hurtful things about me on her blog. There's a small scar on my heart to this day that comes with me when I make friends, and I hear that they have talked about me to others.

My heart races some, my pulse quickens, and I wonder if I can trust them.

I realized again, quite recently, just how much I allow words to affect me.

There are days when the first thought in my mind as I wake up is how tired I am and how much I am looking forward to when I can fall into my bed once more. Want to know something? The rest of my day, I am tired.

There are days when a coworker says in a joking, sarcastic tone something condescending because I am still "new", and I go through the rest of my shift in a slight funk because of this.

There was a time when a friend joked and called me a name. It stung, it hurt, and we didn't talk for a few days.

There are weeks where all I listen to is music that revolves around sex and drugs and curse words. When I go and talk with friends, I drop curses like I'm a sailor. My mind is unclean and it wanders.

But this is a story about what a supervisor once said to me.

When I was finishing with my internship, we had our long-anticipated exit interviews. As I said before, my teammate and I had a bit of a rough time on the road, but our manager said that we were *hard to manage*.

As we sat in the office, before we went on to other things, the last thing my supervisor said to me was this: "Gwen, we were hoping you would pull your teammate up to you, instead, you let her pull you down."

I tried to fight the tears as her words cut into my heart.

How could she say this? Does she even know what it's like? She's never been on the road. She's never been in my shoes. She doesn't understand all the things that happened. She doesn't understand the peace that I tried to make with everything.

But these words changed me after that meeting. I felt broken. I didn't know my truth of what had happened anymore, I only knew what others saw.

When I came home and hung out with Rachel, I told her what happened. I had told her everything since the beginning so she had a heads-up on what was coming. When I told her this, I saw her eyes pain slightly. She knew how much I was affected by this phrase. When I was done telling her everything, with a few tearstains left on my cheek, she said to me, "You know Gwen, I once heard that it's easier for someone to pull you off of a chair than it is for you to pull them up onto it."

Just like that, the crack in my heart stopped digging in. I hadn't thought of that. Here I was blaming myself for all that had gone wrong. For the miscommunication, the misconceptions, the misunderstandings, the mess-ups, and the screw-ups from our time on the road. All of it, I felt like I could have prevented it somehow. But in reality I couldn't.

There is nothing and was nothing that I could do or say to change my supervisor's mind. She had made it up based on everything that had happened that semester. But what I don't know if she realized then (or has), is just how much of an effect on me those words had.

I don't deny that we were rough to work with on the road, it was hard all around, and tensions were high.

So when I heard these words, I allowed them to hold power over me. Powers of shame, uncertainty and discomfort. Truly making me look back at my experience with a filter of the idea that I had not done what I needed to do. But that's not true.

Words hold a power over us all. They define us whether we like it or not. But when our Truth is deeper than these words that we receive or hear, we are able to decipher what it is that belongs in the cracks of our hearts to allow us to grow, what can heal them, and cast them away. Rachel's words helped stop the hurt from reaching and poisoning the roots of what I knew to be true—I had tried.

Chapter Twenty-Four
Friends

I've said it before and I'll say it again, my friends are amazing.

Many of my friends are lifetime friends. They're not only going to be in my life for a long time, but they *have been* in my life for a long time. Because of our history, they know *all* of my history. Sometimes when it's late, and we've had a few drinks or are simply reminiscing, our talks wander from where we are and what is happening to things that happened years ago.

We chat about clothes we wore growing up and how many of those styles are back *in* style.

We laugh about who we had crushes on and also wonder what those guys are up to now.

We laugh about classes that we thought were hard and compare them to college courses we struggled through.

We smile at moments where we were just children, just teenagers, just young adults.

We remember those times that maybe have a picture attached or a tall-tale that is one of those moments that have bonded us forever.

You know those Buzzfeed stories that you tag your friends on Facebook on: How to know if we're lifetime friends? That's my friends and I. We have all the crazy tales to fill up hours of conversations.

Because many of my friends and I have been friends for so long, we grew up together when we were our most vulnerable: middle school and high school.

They've seen me when I was a chubby, little middle school student, when I broke both my feet (at separate times), when I thought it was a good idea to chop off my hair. They've seen me do crazy things, say stupid things, and sometimes just be stupid. They've seen me chase after things I wanted, long for others, and sometimes, very rarely, settle.

Because we have so much history, my friends don't beat around the bush with me. My friends know me for who I am and know when I need to hear something I might not want to hear.

In the spring of 2017, I had just come back from an amazing semester long internship with Thirst Project post-graduation from college, and all anyone ever said to me was, *"So Gwen, what's next?"*

After just a week of hearing this, my best friend Kierstin and I went out for Mexican food, and I told her how frustrated I was by people always asking this.

She looked at me, smiled and said: "Gwen, that's because there is always something next for you. You're always off doing something or working towards some next big thing for yourself. It's natural for us to think it."

I hadn't realized what my life looked like to others until she told me that. It helped me to realize where everyone else's question came from; a spot of pure, honest wonder of what was I going to do next.

Much like you and your friends, my friends and I have had long talks where we end up closing down restaurants. We have texted one another a SOS to talk about problems at home, problems in relationships. We have driven over to one another's houses in the wee hours of the morning just to offer support.

These are just a few of the memories that make my friendships so special.

As I've gotten older, and now that I am out of school, I realize just how hard it can be to make friends in your 20s. When all you do is work, it's hard to maintain the relationships that you already have but also want to create new ones. There's a beautiful truth that I just recently learned: we all want to have friends and be a friend.

I was chatting with some coworkers a few days ago about how we were all wanting to intentionally make time for other women in our lives, how our circles have changed over time, and we want to make sure we have a solid group of female friends. We all smiled and laughed and realized that we all were at that same point in life. We made a decision right there to make sure we made time for one another, and not just in the early hours of the morning when we were getting our store ready for the day.

Around the same time as this conversation with my coworkers, another friend reached out who was having trouble making connections in her small group. In our group chat with a few other girls, we all spoke about our own experiences. Each experience came down to one thought: when you go to an event, any event, remember that everyone there came to make friends. It doesn't matter how large their friend group already is, they still want to connect with other people.

So the next time I get invited to go to a party, or drinks after work, or anything really, especially when I'm not feeling like I truly want to go, I'm remembering how I want to make more friends. I'm remembering how I feel when I invite people to come and do something, and they aren't able to come or don't show up. I'm remembering that we all really just want a few more friends in life. I hope you can remember this too.

Chapter Twenty-Five
Honesty

One of the most beautiful things in life is honesty.

It's a really hard line to cross. Do I tell the truth, the whole truth, and nothing but the truth? Or do I tell the truth but slightly exclude something to not hurt someone's feelings?

It's hard.

Sometimes we have to walk that line of truth. Maybe it's circumstantial, maybe it's personal; either way you have to be careful. We've all been there.

Here's one of the things I love about honesty in my life.

I have one rule when it comes to my friends and our relationships: When they are dating someone, I will tell them my honest opinion one time and one time only, and it's theirs for the liking. Afterwards I will *always* support them.

That's it.

Alright, you're probably laughing at me right? *Gwen, how do you keep your feelings out of it when your friends are making multiple bad decisions? Gwen, what are you talking about? You actually tell them what you think of their lying, cheating boy/girl friend?*

Yes, I value my friendships more than I value my friends choosing my opinion.

My friends have definitely dated their share of crazies; I'm not going to lie. They've also done their share of craziness (and I'm sure they have more coming, just like I do, but that's beside the point.) I *love* my friends so much that I want them to know my honest opinion of whatever is going on in their life. If I think they're about to make a huge mistake doing something, I will tell them. And if (or when) they continue to do whatever it was that I thought was bad, I'll be there for them, offering a hand if they ever need it.

If I have a friend who I think is dating a not-amazing person, I will tell them. If (and when) they continue to date them, I will be there. I will go to the parties and talk to their significant other. I'll get to know them. I'll be there if they fight and offer support. I'll bring over the ice cream when they need a little cry session. I'll be there. I'll share their excitement when they each say, "I love you" for the first time. I'll jump up and down with joy when they start talking about getting married. I'll cry when I see the ring on their finger, knowing they had found their other half.

But I will *never* let my opinions get in the way of being a friend (disclaimer: unless there's something *seriously* wrong.)

And if somehow, my humanness, my pettiness, does get in the way, I have an open door policy. My door is always open to my friends, my family, even those I pass on the street. If we have a falling out, or my friend doesn't like my opinion, my door is always open.

Chapter Twenty-Six
Forgiveness

I got my first *real* job when I was 18. A real job that wasn't working for either of my parents or picking up odd jobs with neighbors. I was working at a florist shop, something that I had always dreamed of doing. I loved working with my hands and creating beautiful art out of living things.

For years I had longed after a reputable flower shop in my town. I wanted to work *there,* but even though I applied, no one really wanted to hire an 18-year-old whose other job experience was simply mowing lawns and tending the flowerbeds of her home. It wasn't until a new, local flower shop came into business that I found my chance to work with flowers.

I stopped in one day on a whim and asked about a job. My mom was with me. I was such a novice. My mom and the owner talked and happened to know each other vaguely from her son and my brother being in school together. I was offered the job right away. Got my license scanned and started the next week.

I was their new flower delivery girl.

I learned to drive a giant van, and made my way around the city after school and on weekends delivering flowers. I loved it, and I hated it.

This was pre-smartphone era for me. I had to find my way while driving a giant beast of a car with MapQuest directions in my right hand all while trying to stay in my lane. I got lost more times than I can count and ended up stopping at many gas stations to use the washroom and ask for directions.

It was not as glamorous as I thought, and the few times I got to arrange flowers was when they would tip over in the back of the van, and I simply set them back in their vases.

My second week on the job, my boss (who was also the owner) went with me on a flower delivery to the local hospital. The flower shop had arranged a contract with the hospital, and she wanted to show me how it all worked. Where I parked, where I took the flowers and picked up the arrangements that didn't sell, and who to hand the forms to. While we were driving, we started discussing wages: how and when I would be paid. *Would it be based off of hours of driving? Would it be based off of deliveries I made? Would it simply be an hourly wage? Would I get tips from customers, and would I have to turn them into her?* These were the things we talked about.

I must say, looking back, I was *very, very* naive. Nowadays, I don't think I would agree to a job unless I knew exactly how and what I was getting paid to do, but then again, this was my *first* job.

Slowly I kept working and slowly the only things I heard about getting paid were, "We'll talk about it," or my favorite, "I'll figure it out soon."

Flash forward after a little over two months of working there, and my friends asked me how it was going. They already had their own jobs or a few under their belts, and we were swapping stories about all the crazy things that happen at work. I offhandedly mentioned how I hadn't been paid yet (I think we were lamenting on minimum wages—oh how funny now!) Both my friends stopped talking and stared at me.

"You haven't gotten paid yet?"

"Do your parents know?"

To me, it didn't seem that odd, I wasn't entirely sure how it was supposed to work.

I told my parents who had asked a few times when and what I was getting paid, and they said I had to talk to my boss.

Around this time, I applied at the first nursery that I had always dreamed of working at. It was *huge,* so much bigger than the small space I was working at now. And I would actually get to work with plants. I would get to tend the seeds, water them, weed them, show patrons which plants would fit their needs, and help with arragements. It seemed perfect.

I went in for an interview (after stopping by *many* times after I dropped off my application, I finally got to talk to the person who did the hiring and the owner! Perseverance and persistence does pay off!). They asked me about my current employment at this other florist. I was honest; I told them that even if they paid me soon, I would be leaving them. I wasn't a fan of how I was being treated or even really what I was doing. It was a good place to get my toes wet but that was it.

They seemed interested, and slightly alarmed by the current situation but offered me the job anyway.

Over the next weeks, I consistently stopped into my old job, I gave my two week notice, and they said just don't come back. I went back with a piece of paper detailing out the numbers of hours I had worked and asking to paid for the time, at minimum wage, nothing more and nothing less. Surprisingly, my boss was never in the store when I came by. I kept coming and kept coming until her son one day spoke rather harshly to me asking me why I kept coming in with that paper, and what in the *hell* did I want. (To be honest, I think his language was a bit harsher and stronger than what I remember.)

I was 18, and I could feel the tears pooling in my eyes. I was *scared*. I didn't understand why someone would get so harsh and rude to such a young girl, let alone why someone wouldn't simply pay me for all the work that I had done.

I thrust the paper at him and told him that I wanted to get paid for the work I had done. It was only right; it was only fair. Bless the heart of the new worker who was standing behind the counter with him, I hoped she learned from this.

I wanted to give it to my boss, but her son was saying that he was now my boss, even though I didn't work there.

To be honest, that is all I really remember of that day. I remember both of us signing my paper saying that I had given it to them and the poor girl standing behind the counter signed it as a witness. I was never paid though, and I saw the pity in her eyes as I walked out with tears rolling down my cheeks unsure what had really just happened.

Months went by at my new job, which I loved and thrived in. I couldn't bring myself to go back to my old 'job' and try and get the money that I deserved from my actual boss. Heck, I could barely bring myself to drive by the building. And when I did, I would flip it off. What can I say? I was mad. I didn't understand how I could have been treated so poorly. It just wasn't right.

Months and years went by. Oftentimes my parents would bring up that I should say something to the local paper and get authorities involved because it was technically illegal the work that I did (At the time being 18, I shouldn't have been driving nor working the hours I did there, especially not getting paid and not being under their insurance). But I never did.

Some said that I should sue to get what I deserved, but I never did.

A few years later, my mom and I were out grocery shopping, and she stopped in the checkout line saying she thought she saw my old boss. My insides tightened, and I wanted to run. I didn't want to face her. My mom, being the mother bear, always wished she had given her a piece of her mind.

As we were driving home that day, I realized that I didn't want to run from her any more. I wanted to be able to, if I saw her one-day, to go up and say "I forgive you for what happened. I won't forget it, I may have forgotten some of the details, but I forgive you."

I didn't want to hold a grudge any longer. I had stopped flipping off the building partly because the shop went under and partly because I no longer cared. I had become numb.

I don't know how I did it. I really think much of it was time and working somewhere where I was valued and knew that I was a part of a team that was doing wonderful things.

At some point I thought I saw my boss out and about in town, and I knew that I could go up to her and say that I had forgiven her. I wish this was one of those stories that had step-by-step instructions on how to go about forgiveness, and I'm sorry that it's not. I know I was angry, hurt, sad, and scared. Then I was defiant toward their business. Then I was timid to even see them or their arrangements. *Finally* I realized I no longer wanted to be so, and I had to change.

I am not a proponent for saying that any ill will that happens between people is water under the bridge when it is resolved. Perhaps in small things, but when they are large enough to cause strife, there is something to learn there.

I learned *so much* from my first job. I learned that I need to know exactly what it is I will be doing and how I will be compensated for my job. I learned that I need to get along with those I work for, not just have a fantasy in mind of what it will look like. I learned that I need to be a part of a team and feel valued as I work there.

So, Tracy (I think that was your name), if I were to meet you anywhere in the world right now, I don't wish you ill will. I am (slightly) sorry that your business went under. But, I forgive you for what happened. I forgive you for treating me so badly, for getting mad at me that I wouldn't buy a cellphone that had a GPS. I forgive you for sending me, an 18-year-old girl, around a city with nothing more than MapQuest directions. I forgive you for lying to me about what the job would be like, for how I would be paid, and for literally everything that happened. Hell, I even forgive your son who was so rude to me. But I hope you don't take my forgiveness as forgetfulness. I have never let anyone speak to me the way you or your son did. I am worth more than that. I have never signed a contract or been hired when I don't know all the details, especially how I will be paid for my services. I have never gotten a job that I don't think will actually help me in the long run or will simply be good for the time being. I will never forget what happened; yes I may forget some of the details, but you helped shape me the way I am today. Please, please do not take this forgiveness and think that all is dandy on what happened. It's not. I truly hope and pray that *no one* that comes to your business, the flower shop or any others you wish to create, is *ever* treated the way that I was. Just imagine if the roles were reversed.

Chapter Twenty-Seven
Community

Being 23 and living at home is hard. Along with not being in school and working full-time, it makes finding friends even harder. Something happens in your 20s when you realize just who is really in your corner, who you want to have in your corner, and how you want to bring people into it.

Something that is amazingly powerful to keep in mind when you're making friends in your 20s is that we are *not* meant to live this life alone. Think of the disciples, here was a ragtag group of young people who weren't chosen to go into school. In fact they were the ones that those in the schools thought wouldn't make it, so they became fishermen.

And guess who Jesus chose to be a part of His community? He didn't go straight to the churches and grab the pastors to be His friends, *nope*. He went to the docks and grabbed the workers, those that weren't chosen to go into ministry. That's who He chose to be in His corner.

I have many friends in my life who have been here for years. I've had many friends who have been in my life for a season. From the World Race to doing a two-week mission trip to England, to college, to being home, to a semester-long internship, to being home once more, people have fluttered in and out of my life like the wind.

There have been many changes, but also many things have stayed the same when it comes to becoming friends and creating memories.

There have been team times where we go and explore a city and take amazingly artsy photos that are extremely double-tap-worthy.

We have eaten crazy new foods and tried to learn the language of wherever we are. We have even stayed up watching *Friends* or making giant beds and watching movies all day long.

We've stood on balconies and watched as people paraded by to a festival. We've sat and talked deeply about where we are in life and what we want. We've sung, danced, laughed, and cried together.

We've been in the car for months or sometimes just hours. We've been silent, and we've been rowdy. We've gone on adventures near and far. We've seen the world and parts of our own city together. We've stayed up late getting coffee and cookies, Taco Bell, crumpets.

We've made memories.

Many of my friends are at different points in their lives. Some are married. Some are working hard to make their way in the world. Some are stay-at-home moms. Some are working multiple jobs to make ends meet. But no matter where my friends are in their lives, we have always been able to find time for each other.

Whether we are all working crazy hours or the usual 9-5, almost every Monday night I am at Rachel's house watching *The Bachelor* or *Bachelorette*. Or we're texting each other during the entire show.

At least every two weeks, Kierstin and I get Mexican food, eat ice cream, and watch a movie.

At least once a week, I stop in and see Ashley at work.

At least every day, I am texting Kierstin, Rachel, and Stacy.

At least once a month, Stacy and I talk on the phone.

Every few weeks, Kellen and I call and catch up.

Every few weeks, Cole and I will get coffee and adventure.

Every few weeks, Erin and I will at least get coffee and then plan an adventure for the following week.

Every two months, I catch up with my friends in England.

Every few weeks Ashley and I get lunch together.

Every few weeks Cheyenne, Ashley, and I have a girls night.

Every few weeks, Moni and I catch up over Facebook Messenger.

We've found ways to keep one another in our lives forever.

We may not be in college anymore and able to stay up until 3AM and still make it to class the next day, and the coffee shops around us might close up at 10PM, but we still know how to make sure that every person in our lives feels like a priority, because they are.

Chapter Twenty-Eight
You Are Worthy

Sometimes it takes a while for something to sink in. For me, no matter how much my friends tell me something, I have to come to terms with it on my own and fully understand it before it actually clicks in my brain.

It took me a while to realize this, and I suppose it's partly due to some of the stubbornness I have in me. When it came to one of my best friends, it took even longer to realize how I was no longer a major priority in his life.

We had a bit of an odd history. We became fast friends, more like family. Talking about the deep stuff of our lives: our struggles, our dreams, our plans, and our hopes. It was bliss. He became a crutch during a few harder times of life. I knew I could always reach out to him if I needed something. He would be there. Until, slowly he wasn't.

It was late fall when I finally got to see him again in person. It seemed like we still clicked, I knew he was in my corner, but something felt off, like instead of taking a seat, he was almost lingering on the sidelines, inching to get away. I didn't think much of it until we started missing one another.

We used to talk every few weeks and text in between. We would catch one another up on life and all that was going on. One weekend we were set to brainstorm ideas for the upcoming year. I had gone to work that morning knowing I would be talking to my best friend that afternoon and couldn't have been happier. When I clocked out at work and looked at my phone, nothing was there from him. It hurt a bit, but I let it slide, *again*. I figured he was busy. I went on and saw some friends, went out to eat and the next day went back to work. Still *nothing*. So I went and saw my family like usual, and then went out with some friends.

Monday rolled around and *nothing* again. You're probably wondering, *Gwen, why didn't you just call him? Hello!* Well here's the thing: Recently I had always been the one to call. And I didn't want to be anymore. I wanted this friendship to be two ways, and it no longer was.

It hurt to realize this. I felt like part of my heart was being split, was being torn from my chest and going with him. I felt like I could no longer go to him to tell him the good, the bad, or the ugly. I didn't know what to do, but I knew I could no longer *run* this friendship.

A few months later he reached out, saying how sorry he was that he lost track of time over the holidays and wanted to catch up. I answered almost right away and realized how I truly knew nothing that was going on his life, just as he knew nothing about mine. While trying to be upbeat and happy that we were talking again, I imagined what it would possibly be like to see him in person.

I cringed inwardly thinking about how awkward it most likely would be! Only talking about the past, asking one another questions, the most basic of questions like "Where are you living now? What exactly is your job again?" Because neither of us knew anymore.

You see, he was such a major part of my life for so long, I loved it. It was magic with him there. He encouraged me and helped me grow more than I thought possible. While at the moment, he's on the sidelines, I hope and pray that he will come back in and take a seat once more in my corner. But I had to do what was best for me. I could no longer put out the same amount of effort, time, and energy that I had been giving out in our friendship. I could no longer make him as much of a priority when it was to not be reciprocated.

Sure, I do hope that one day he'll reciprocate, and all will be well once more, but it's ok if it's not. It's okay that we fell apart. It's okay that he's no longer my go-to person. It's okay that we don't know where the other is. Sure, when we see each other again, we'll have a lot to catch up on, which may be slightly awkward but will be some good conversations.

I hope you know just how valued you are, friend. I knew it before this friendship fizzled, but I know it more so now. It's okay if someone wants to walk away. The reason why is because you need someone who will be there through it all. Even if they say so, they need to mean it, they need to show it. You deserve people who know *all* the details of your life, not just the headlines.

Chapter Twenty-Nine
Old Habits Die Hard

When I was growing up, I was often sick. Sometimes it was just your average cold that lasted way longer than normal. Others it was a broken bone. And then there were my allergic reactions without any common cause and migraines.

By the time junior high rolled around, I had a nickname, the sick girl. I remember when I cracked my growth plate in my left arm and people would comment, "You got hurt, again?" with a sneering lip, looking down at the cast on my arm. It just seemed to be inevitable. I was the sick girl. I would always be the sick girl.

As high school came around, I got sick with migraines. I remember it was orientation day. My two best friends and I went together to get our schedules, find our lockers, and make our ways around the building. As the day was coming to a close, I was feeling really sick. My head was pounding. I felt shaky and weak. My mom figured it was low blood sugar, so we went out to eat afterwards. That's when I got *really* sick. I vomited in the restaurant and raced out of the building and continued to get sick on the sidewalk. My head was reeling with a pain I had never experienced before.

Two years went by of not being able to fully attend school. Of going to doctor after doctor searching for the cause, trying different kinds of medications, and missing out of being a kid.

I slowly started getting better my junior year of high school, but my future was unbelievably uncertain. I still missed school. I had a designated "rest" period built into my schedule, and I was still going to the doctor at least once a week to get treated.

My future was completely up in the air, but I was determined to graduate high school, even though my records showed that though I was considered a junior, my credits rested just above being a freshman. Advisors and teachers encouraged me to stay an extra year. Doctors suggested it too, even saying that I should wait to apply to college. I didn't. I graduated with the rest of my class and went onto college.

I still had sick days my first two years. Every so often I would miss a class, but my professors understood, and I still got my work done.

While on the World Race, it was the same as college. Every so often a day would come where my head would ache too much to get out of bed. I decided three months into my journey to stop taking my medicine; to this day I haven't taken my migraine medicine. Every so often I will have a migraine, but one that will be fixed with some over-the-counter pain pills and rest.

As college came to a close, most of my illnesses did too. My migraines were almost fully gone as were my allergies. I had hardly ever had an allergic reaction since I was in Asia in 2015. Thai culture uses *tons* of fish and shellfish, and I reacted to it almost the entire month. It was extremely difficult, and I even had to go to the hospital once for a shot.

I'll never forget lying in bed with a fan blowing on me and my teammate laying on the floor next to my bed watching movies with me. I barely had the energy to talk, let alone go to the bathroom, so we sat in silence most days. I felt like an invalid and didn't know what to do. Scenes flashed through my mind of the taunts and comments that I dealt with growing up.

"She's sick—again."

"How are you always sick?"

"You missed this, again."

"I suppose I can give you an extension."

"How are you ever going to graduate?"

I never prayed so hard in my life that month as I did for healing in Thailand. It came, eventually, but I still had to be cautious. I lived off 7/11 the whole month, cups of yogurt and packaged nuts.

When I got my allergic reaction out of the blue in 2017, I didn't know what to think. I couldn't figure out what had caused it. All I had done the days before were make Christmas ornaments with a coworker and then had dinner with friends.

When I woke up, my face was swollen. I missed a week of work. I felt weak. I was sick again.

I wondered if I would ever fully be well once more. Not a month later, I woke up with a red and puffy eye. The days before I visited a friend's house, and the night before I had dinner with another friend. It was uncanny just how similar the days before were to each reaction.

I sat in my kitchen crying over my breakfast. *"Why Lord? Why now? Why again? I thought I was healthy. What in the world caused this? Am I allergic to something new? Do I need to get more tests done? Do I need to be more careful?"*

I didn't know anything except that I was angry. I was frustrated. I was mad. I was sad.

I walked around my house that morning crying, yelling, and sobbing as I wondered what to do. But one thought overshadowed them all: I thought I was healthy.

I *am* healthy. I *know* God has healed me from my migraines. I *know* God will fully heal me from my crazy reactions. But I also know that I am not the porcelain doll that I once was. Whenever I get even the slightest sickness I am overcome with the shame of what it was like growing up, always being sick. Hearing the whispers behind my back, murmurs on everything that was going on.

But at 24, I am probably the healthiest I have ever been. I can go to work regularly, I can see friends, I can go to movies, I can go out, I can travel. I can do anything, not having to really worry about my health. Sometimes I think it is so hard to remember that we are no longer who we once were. I think of it with family that I don't see very often. Whenever a family member sees you after a while of not seeing you, they usually exclaim, "My! Look at you!" Because in their minds, we are still little.

I think this is what happens to how we see ourselves too. When I started getting my reactions again, I thought of myself as the young girl who was always sick and missed out on so much of life. But I'm not anymore. It may have taken me 10 plus years to fully remove that label, but it is finally gone.

Maybe you struggled with your health like I have. Maybe you struggled in school too, or maybe you were bullied.

We can shred those labels, they don't have to stay and hang over us.

We only need to go to God about it. Let His truths flood who we have let others say that we are.

I am not sick. I am wonderfully made.

I am not ugly. I am beautifully made.

I am not stupid. I am weaved with wisdom.

I am not unworthy. I am worthy.

I am not unlovable. I am loved.

I am not weak. I am strong in the Lord.

I am enough.

Chapter Thirty
Foundation

When I came home from my internship, I was shattered. I was tired. I was unsure of what I wanted to do. I was hurt. I was lonely. I was skeptical. I was strung out.

The best word I found: spent. It perfectly encapsulated all that I was feeling.

After months of trying to figure out what I wanted to do and not getting any closer to what it was than when I flew home, I emailed my squad mentor from the World Race.

I laid it all out before him, where I was at, what I was feeling, and how lost I felt.

He responded quite promptly and sent his condolences first on where I was at and continued to share ways that I could work to understanding and forgiving all that had happened.

A few weeks afterwards, we chatted on the phone. I was heading into Target to get my niece her birthday gift and a few groceries. As soon as I was at the bread aisle, Ben asked me, "Gwen what's your purpose?" I laughed looking for the delicious, multi-seed, gluten-free bread.

"Ben, you're going to make me cry in the middle of Target!"

As we continued to talk, and I told him what I was feeling, he spoke so much truth into my soul right there. He asked me, "What is the thing that you can pursue that puts you in an environment that lets you learn the things the Lord is asking to you to do?"

The answer to this, I still do not know. I wasn't sure what Ben was going to tell me that day, but I knew it was something that I needed to hear. It was something that my soul needed to be fed to break through the protective soundproof wall I had built up in order not to get hurt once more but to flourish again under the sun.

One of the things that made me stop my cart right by the luggage was this:

"If everything is important then nothing is actually important."

Wow. What wisdom. Suddenly I realized all of my to-do lists, all the things I wanted to get done on my days off, afternoons off work, mornings when I go in late seemed pointless. Sure clean clothes are great, but if I'm using the time to do laundry that I should be using to do something else, like spending time with God, then something needed to change. Which is how we got to the issue of my foundation.

Over the last few months, I rested. I needed rest. I was *spent*. But now had come the time for me to stop resting and start the work.

I think of it as a garden. As fall rolls around, my garden beings to die. The weather wears and tears at the plants, and they can't flourish under the wind and cooler temperatures, so they die. You pull them out, lay some mulch and new nutrient rich soil on the ground, and prepare for winter.

As winter comes, the ground rests in a different way than the rest of the seasons. It's preparing for the next plant. Me, in my winter season, I've simply been resting. Now I must prepare for the next plant, because as spring comes, I need to weed my foundation and allow for the proper things to flourish.

I have allowed my foundation to get some cracks and those cracks have filled with a love of Netflix, self-indulgence, disregard for my body and health, and a few other things. These aren't terrible, and I'm not going to die tomorrow because of them, but they sure do make my days harder.

In this season of restoring my foundation, I am making a conscious effort to work on myself. Not just exercise, but all around being a better human being.

Since Ben and I are so alike, he warned me not to make to-do lists of what to work on.

"Take it day by day and breath by breath. Give yourself proper freedom that you can function in. Get high and hard accountability. Tell them, this is what the Lord has asked me to do, this is where I struggle, these are my limits."

If I were to make a to-do list of everything I wanted to do in a day it would read something like this:

Watch the sunrise

Do a devotional

Go for a run

Eat a healthy breakfast

Listen to good music on the way to work

Work hard, excel, be friendly, enjoy it

Come home

Read a book (maybe watch an episode of a show)

Spent time with family

Go to bed

But you see, when I read that, I see all the *things* that I wish to do rather than the One who gave me the day.

I set to work. Not on my to-do lists, but on my days and how I spent them. I started doing a devotional each day. I make a conscious effort to start my days with one. Even when I work an opening shift, I bring my devotional with me to do on my break. I am making an effort to work out more during the week, to take walks, to take care of my body. I stopped binge watching on Netflix (sort of, *Riverdale* was just so captivating!). I would have shows on in the background while I worked on other things, but I didn't just sit and watch. I stopped wasting hours scrolling through social media, comparing my life to others.

I am setting the foundation for what I want my life to be like twenty years from now. I want to be a healthy, God-loving woman. If I'm not that now, how will I be then?

Ben's last bit of advice:

"We have to solidify the foundation to be able to accept the weight that is coming." Are you ready?

Chapter Thirty-One

Seasons

I think that we all go through different seasons of life. Some are only a few days long, others last months or even years. Some are easy and breezy, full of fun moments and laughter. Some are the hardest and darkest moments of our lives.

These are my seasons.

Winter

Winter is absolutely beautiful. I love when the first snow falls; I get giddy in anticipation of seeing the bright, white, soft snow covering everything.

It's beautiful.

Winter to me, is a time of rest. I long for curling up on the couch with a good book, underneath a comfy blanket, and just spending time being. Winter is also *full* to the brim of holiday activities, which makes my heart happy with being able to see family and friends.

Winter can be rough though. Even though everything has burrowed inside to rest for the springtime, the elements outside are harsh on you. Whenever my friends want to make plans that involve being outdoors, I pack on the layers. Thick winter tights under leggings under jeans with three pairs of socks and a tank top, t-shirt, long sleeve, sweater, and finally a coat. It's a miracle I can move with all the layers I have on.

It's protection against it all.

In my winter months, I long to just be with those that I love. My family, my friends, to be surrounded by cheery faces perhaps even surrounding a warm blazing fire.

Winter isn't meant for us to seek solitude always, winter is meant for us to recoup ourselves so that we can do better when the snow melts.

Spring

Every year when my dad and I plant some flowers around our house, he makes a *huge* deal about when they start to bloom. I swear he walks around the outside of the house every morning and night just to see if you can spot the little shoots of the flowers. As soon as he does, he comes racing back in and calls for us to come out and see them too. To realize that winter is over, spring has truly sprung.

Spring is a glorious season. It's a season of preparation, anticipation, and expectations.

Spring is the season that allows for the bloom of summer.

Spring is the season where I get to work in my garden. After the harsh winter, I have to start to nurture the soil back to health. I pull weeds, I water, I till the soil, add in fertilizer. The winter has allowed for all the nutrients to set and be ready to be used, so now I spread it all out and start to work for what is to come.

Spring is one of the most demanding seasons but in a truer sense of the work being done.

Spring is the season where you will look back on and realize all that you actually did, all that hard work truly paid off.

Summer

I am a summer girl. My mom *loves* to share the story of how when I was a baby and loved to be swaddled (much like I do even now. This girl loves her blankets.) She would wrap me up, take me outside, and sing, "My little summer girl" as she rocked me under the summer sun.

Summer is beautiful. Summer is relaxing. Summer is full of life.

I love how the seasons follow one another. Spring is a season of hard work and dedication and summer is the fruit of your labors.

You can see how all of your hard work has paid off. You can look out and see a garden full and blooming of all of your favorite fruits and vegetables.

You're able to take time and rest from school and work. You're able to go on vacations and explore.

Summer is a season of fruit, a big juicy bowl of the best strawberries you have ever had.

Summer is one of my favorite times of the year.

Fall

I love fall.

I love all the colors, the way the weather changes, the way my heart feels, fall leaves.

I just can't help but stare in wonder at the all the trees and their changing colors. It seemed like just a few days ago they were all bright green, and I was wearing shorts and a tank top, and we were heading to the pool. Now I was bundled and the trees were bundling inside, getting ready for winter.

As I stared at the leaves, I distinctly heard God whisper in my ear, "*Just as the leaves draw in their nutrients for the coming months, what are you drawing deep into your soul?*"

This hit me so hard. *What am I drawing into my soul? What does this next season mean for me? How am I wanting to grow?*

I don't have the answers, but I know one thing without a doubt: I want to stop *hurrying*. I want to be able to sit and enjoy a cup of coffee without looking at my watch. I want to enjoy stopping to talk with a friend I haven't seen in awhile without having to worry about being late for work. I want to go out with my family and enjoy my time with them and not worry about all the work that is still waiting of me to finish.

Here's what I am going to do:

I'm going to stop planning all that I have to get done. It's overwhelming, to be honest, and just makes me stressed. I'm going to live each day as it comes. Sure I'll still plan to do things, but I'm not going to plan every moment of the day until I fall into bed too weary to even enjoy a meal.

As the holidays are quickly approaching, think about what you are taking into your soul for the next few months. Maybe it's preparation in seeing family, or a change of a job or location. Whatever it is, set yourself up well for what is to come. Make time for the small things, like watching the sunrise; but don't forget to take time for yourself, for your soul.

Chapter Thirty-Two
Thread Memory

Do you ever find it hard to give away your clothes?

The other day I woke up determined to purge my closet. It's a feeling I get a few times a year, usually around the start of a new season. I look at all the clothes that I have and pull them out of my closet one by one.

I hold them up and ask, "Did I wear you?" if the answer is no, I throw it into the give-away box. If the answer is only once, I ask myself, "Will I wear you again?" and sometimes throw it in the give-away and sometimes in the maybe. If I love it and wear it all the time, I put it in the keep pile.

I have these milk crates that hold *tons* of old t-shirts of mine. Some were from high school, many from college, and a handful of ones that I've picked up on my travels. Every time I go to clean out my closet I get stuck on these.

I hardly ever wear them, and if I do it's only to the gym. Even then, I still hardly wear them, but I keep them.

I have this one zippered jacket that I got back in college at a resale store. It quickly became my favorite jacket. I wore it pretty much every day. It had a small little hole on one of the elbows when I first got it, but in the years and places I have worn it, that hole now covers my entire elbow and then some. There are pit stains all the way down to the band at the waist and there are many, many stains. But I can't bring myself to get rid of it.

Why? You ask, well this jacket has been with me through tons of memories. This jacket was with me during the season where we would travel up to Chicago to see Noah and his family. Heck, I think I actually got it up there.

This jacket was with me when I was trying to decipher what God had for me, to go onto the mission field or to stay at school.

This jacket came with me around the world.

This jacket helped ease my reentry, tied around my waist.

This jacket came with me back to school, like a blanket, always there, always reminding me of what was and what will be.

This jacket has seen tears of joy and deep sorrow. This jacket has seen praise from the rooftops of the Dominican Republic to the beaches of South Africa. This jacket has seen excitement at getting the dean's list and rejection at not getting a job.

This jacket has been there through it all.

Now it is all threadbare, but I still can't bring myself to get rid of it. Even now as I type this, I long to pull on the sleeves and be reminded of all that we have done together.

It can sometimes seem silly to be so attached to something that is easily replaced; but I don't think so, it just makes it hard to say goodbye when the time comes.

That day, after I purged so much from my closet, I raced my clothes over to Goodwill before I could change my mind. I gave them *everything* in the basket, all the t-shirts, sweaters, pants, and shorts, and when I came home I felt good, liberated even.

When I woke up the next day, I had a deep regret and sorrow building in my chest. There was a pair of Thai pants in that basket that I gave away. A pair that a dear friend had given me on the Race but I had not worn in over 3 years. I knew I would probably never wear them, which is why I gave them away, but now that they no longer lived in my closet with the possibility of me wearing them, it seemed too great to think about.

I honestly *love* getting rid of my stuff. It's weird thing to like, I know, but it makes me feel so free and happy knowing that it's just material objects, and they can be replaced. But when I woke up that morning I was so sad that I hadn't thought to keep it. I *knew* I would never wear them, I knew that, but without having their presence in my closet, I missed them.

For some reason, before big life changes, I almost always go and get a new pair of shoes. This last pair of shoes I bought were a pair of grey Chucks. I love them. They remind me of high school and early college, and after all the adventures I have had in them, I am reminded of the miles we have traveled together.

Whenever the time comes that I have to get a new pair of shoes, my heart will break when I throw those away. We had so many wonderful times together, we have seen so many things, achieved so much, and now we are saying goodbye.

It can seem crazy, but I bet you, there's a reason why you have a favorite sweater or a favorite pair of jeans in your closet. I am sure part of it is the fit, but what about the memories in them? What about that pair of jeans you wore during an amazing dinner you had with your friends that seemed to last only a few minutes because it was so great, but really you sat at the restaurant until they closed? Or that sweater you wore when you told your boyfriend you loved him?

There are events that happen in our clothes that help make them so special to us. That jacket, (I went and put it on by the way, it doesn't match but that's OK) will probably live in my closet for *years*, and every time I wear it, I'll feel a little nostalgic, very blessed, and excited for what is to come.

Chapter Thirty-Three
Choose Fearless

One of the biggest, and arguably, most important lessons I have learned about vulnerability is:

Never apologize for wanting the most out of your life.

I've told you a bit about my brother, and no matter how much I love him, it's hard to talk with him sometimes simply because he sees things so opposite from me. Whenever I am at a point in my life where I want to chase after something that might not lead me into a job with a steady paycheck and a 401K match, Noah asks me, *what are you doing that is helping you work towards your future?* My answer is always, I'm not sure, but I know it's worth it.

Many of my friends have chosen a different life path than me. Many are married or in a serious relationship and working in their chosen field or even going back to school to be able to open more doors in a field they want to pursue. It's amazing really, but my life is nothing like theirs.

In September of 2016, Rachel and I were meeting for coffee down by our school. I had just been accepted into an amazing internship with Thirst Project for January, right after I had graduated, and I was starting to get scared about going. So many of my friends were settling down in the Indianapolis area, and I didn't want to miss out. I *almost* wanted to settle. I remember sitting in that coffee shop, sipping my tea, and telling Rachel all of this. She sat there and listened to me, and then told me something along the lines of, "That's not what you're supposed to do."

And she's right.

I'm not the kind of person who dreams of what my future house will look like, of how the backyard will be. I'm the kind of person who dreams of continuing to see the world and all that is out there; of meeting new people, hearing their stories, and being able to share their stories with the world. That's what I dream of doing.

Just this past week, Ashley and I were at lunch, and she asked me how long she thought I would be working at Starbucks. I had no answer, because even a year from now, I don't know exactly what I want to do. I told her, "In a year, I would love to be writing full-time if I can. I would love to have gone back to England, maybe even lived there or preparing to live there for a stint. But I don't know where exactly or what I'll be doing."

I dream of continuing to look back at all that I have been blessed enough to do and let that propel me in wanting to do even more.

I dream of sharing my story with others, a young 20-something that has been able to see much of the world and wants to see more. A young 20-something that wants to change the world for the better. A young 20-something sharing her story and letting others know that it's okay to take the road less traveled. In fact, it needs to be *encouraged*.

Many of the *defining* moments of my life have been moments where I have stepped out of fear and into faith.

When I spent a semester in Washington, DC, I stepped out of the fear of not knowing my roommates, of being the youngest, of not knowing what I was doing, of being scared of messing up, of having never lived in a different city, of not knowing anyone out there.

When I was about to go on the World Race, I stepped out of the possible fear of not finishing college, of not getting an education, of leaving home for the first time for a long time, of leaving the United States for the first time.

When I went to England, I stepped out of the fear of possibly losing my job, of England not living up to the hype, of not knowing anyone I was going with or who I staying with.

When I got an internship with Thirst Project, I stepped out of the fear of not knowing my teammates, not knowing anyone at the company, not liking to drive long distances, and especially being scared to drive in the mountains and bad weather, of leaving my friends and family yet again.

Each one of these moments and many more came when I stepped out of the fear of what could be and stepped into the faith and fearlessness of wanting to live. I learned so much more than I ever thought was possible on the side of fear.

I learned in DC that I can live on my own, and I thrive. I learned how to make friends and how to conduct myself professionally, and most importantly I learned some of what sets my soul on fire. I got over my fear of going places by myself. I wandered the city every hour of the day, taking in the sights and being a tourist at times. I made friends at church; I went by myself to start and then met up with friends. I got involved in groups, and I even attended house parties with my new friends.

When I went on the World Race, I learned how to make friends, I learned a deep appreciation for others, I learned who I am in Christ and just how small this big world can be. I learned not to put limits on God.

When I went to England I learned how connected we all are.

I learned in Los Angeles and in the United States who is in my corner and how to connect with others. I learned how passionate I am about crises that plague our world. I learned that speaking in front of others isn't all that scary. I learned that so many of us long to be a part of something more than just ourselves.

If I had stayed in the fear of the unknown, I wouldn't have been able to experience all that I have in my 20-some years of life. I would have stayed right where I was, stagnant, not growing.

Instead, there have been a few seasons where I have stayed where I am, not due to fear, but due to needing to rest and learn more where my roots are than where I want my roots to transfer.

My hope for you is to live fearlessly. There's a reason I have Fearless tattooed on my foot, I want to walk in it every day of my life. I don't want to be held back by fear.

I hope you do too.

Section Three

Dream

My life has been full of adventure, perhaps not all twenty-some years, but especially the most recent ones have been adventure after adventure.

When I was 19, I went to college. When I was 20, I spent a semester in Washington, DC. When I was 21, I spent a year traveling the world. When I was 22, I spent a few weeks in the UK. When I was 23, I spent a semester traveling the United States.

When I was 23, I was spending my spring break in Washington, DC catching up with friends and exploring the beautiful city. While I was there, I realized just how much I love adventure. I fall in love with cities more and more each time I get to explore them. After having spent so many weeks memorizing shortcuts to my favorite restaurants, shops, and coffee spots, I came back to them with a new light. I was in between adventures but didn't know that one would be coming my way so quickly. I had to change my perspective for what I was doing, I could no longer look at my life in a way of waiting for the next adventure to come or searching for one that I can go on.

I changed my perspective to searching for the magical in the mundane. As I began to look at my life this way, I realized that I was no longer going to allow moments to pass by. I didn't want to waste any time. I wanted to truly live my life to the fullest.

Chapter Thirty-Four
Adventure Awaits

On the top of my right foot is a tattoo of a compass with the words "Adventure Awaits" in between the points. When I got this done when I was 21, it was one of my first tattoos. I had decided I never wanted my life to be boring; I wanted my life to be full of adventure.

As each day comes in the morning, I want to wake up and see that I have a new day ahead of me. Not one that is simply full of a nine-to-five, of work, of commitments. But one that is full of enjoying and celebrating life.

I have a plaque in my room with the renowned quote by Henry David Thoreau, "Dreams are the touchstones of our character." I see it daily; it sits right on top of my bookshelf. I truly believe that dreams are a part of who we are. When we seek to dream, our dreams become a part of who we are and what we are working towards.

Dream until your dreams become a reality and then dream some more.

You see, in my 20-some years of life, they have truly been anything but boring. I have sought out anything but ordinary life.

Have you seen *Beauty & the Beast*? The opening song, *Provincial Life*, Belle sings of how "Each day like the one before. Little town, full of little people....Every morning just the same, since the morning that we came, to this poor provincial town...There must be more than this provincial life!" This is how I sought to live mine once I finished high school. I knew there was something more out there than what I saw and what I knew, and I've been chasing it ever since.

Chapter Thirty-Five
Travel

I am a millennial. I fall into many categories that articles claim that millennials are: I love avocado toast, I love coffee, I love wine, I love to travel. Millennials, and the generations after us, are wired differently because of how connected we are with access to the rest of the world. We have grown up with thoughts of traveling the world and seeing what is out there. Much like many others in their 20s, I have a world map on one of my walls with pins in each place I have been and where I want to go.

At my open house when I graduated from high school, I had a poster for my 'Plan A' life, going to university and obtaining a degree. My 'Plan B' consisted of me traveling the world and seeing all that was out there. Though I started at university, come my junior year of college, God called me off of the school path and onto the path of missions and travel. I embarked on the World Race, an 11-month mission trip to 11 different countries in January of 2015. Having never traveled outside of the United States before, I was in for a rollercoaster of a ride on culture shock, travel, and experiences.

It seemed as though almost every place we went, my heart fell in love with the area. There were others where my heart broke when we had to leave. There were places where I was insanely joyous as the month came to a close, and we went onto our next location. I learned so much during my year, but one of the things I learned the most was just how much I love to travel.

During my mid 20s I spent a few weeks of the summer in England and Wales. I got connected with a team that was going to volunteer and help at a church in a small town on the harbor. We would be working in the city center, performing songs and spoken word pieces. We would be getting to know those in the city that both went to the church and those that didn't. I was able to stay a few extra days and got to make deeper connections with my hosts and friends of the church. I traveled into London and many other towns, exploring from dawn until way past dusk. I was even able to take a day trip with friends to surf in Wales. When I came home, a few weeks later, I started my final semester of school, then a few short months later, I graduated university. Then I was off spending a semester traveling across North America for my dream internship educating the next generation on the global water crisis.

There is something so beautiful that I have sought after in other countries that is in fact in my own. America is truly a melting pot; it is diverse in its range of climates, people, and landscapes all on one continent.

Much of what I have learned on my travels can be found in these pages.

I have learned who I truly am, both in the Lord and this world.

I have learned how to make friends at truck stops, order lines, and each city and town I have been able to pass through.

I have learned what is really important, whether it is making sure I talk to my parents and family or perhaps just my favorite shirt that I brought with me.

I have learned who is important in my life, both those that I am currently with and those that are back home that I miss.

I have learned who is rooting for me to succeed and who sometimes isn't.

I have learned how to be present in each day.

I've learned how to disconnect even when I wish to stay in touch with those away from me.

I have learned how to make moments into memories.

Chapter Thirty-Six
Moments to Memories

Some of my most precious memories from my travels are those that I did not document with a camera.

In the fall of 2013, I was packing to go home for Thanksgiving from Washington, DC. I wanted to take a lot of my summer things with me home so that my travels back at the end of the semester would be a bit easier. I remember hopping out of the shower to missed calls from my friends inviting me to a movie later that evening. I gave them my card number to order my ticket as I was pulling my jeans on and grabbing my shoes to meet them. An hour or so later we had finally made it to Chinatown and were watching the newest *Hunger Games* movie. I didn't get back to my apartment until the wee hours of the morning. I almost slept through my alarm to catch the first metro to the airport. I almost missed my flight, but let me tell you, that night was so worth it.

In the summer of 2014, Rachel and I had just moved into our new dorm room together. We were so excited officially to be roommates! We decided that there was no better way to start out the semester of us living together than by getting on the rooftop of our building. We bounded up the stairs, disregarded the warning sign, and wandered out onto the roof. We could see *everything*. It was unbelievably fun seeing campus from a bird's-eye view.

In May of 2015, I was a part of an all-girls team in Guatemala. We had an entire weekend off and were planning on going to Lake Atitlan, one of the wonders of the world. Many people travel from all over the world to see the crystal blue water and cliff jump. We were unable to figure out a way to travel there and stay, so instead we stayed in our house, watching movies all day long. We brought down all of our mattresses, blankets, and pillows and made one giant bed. We ordered pizza, laughed, cried at the movies, and were just girls enjoying one another's time. It was one of the best moments of my life.

In August of 2015, three friends and I were sitting on the balcony of our homestay right outside Manila in the Philippines, and we played cards for a good four hours. Hour after hour we would switch up the games, sometimes even learning new ones. We sat, talked, laughed, drank tea and water, even had a few cookies. I couldn't tell you what it was that we talked about late into the night, but it was just perfect.

In July 2016, my team and I were in Bristol, England about to go to the annual Harbour Festival. We had been going from sunup to sundown each and every day. We were not truly tired yet, thanks to prayer, but we were on the brink of it. We were resting and suddenly one of us grabbed a guitar and started to play. We all joined in and started singing, worshiping, on the balcony, in the living room, all together in one voice lifted high. It was one of the most pure moments of love and worship I have ever been a part of.

In January of 2017, I was talking to my team in our tiny apartment in Los Angeles telling them about my friends back home. One of my teammates asked if I had pictures of them, and he graciously sat through 20 minutes of me showing photos and telling stories about who was in each photo and where they were and how we knew one another.

In late January of 2017, all four of us interns went to the Griffith Observatory to see the sunset and check out the moon. Turns out all the way at the top of that hill, you barely have cell service. It also turns out that when they close right after sundown, they close the gates coming up to the top. So if you're from out of town, like we were, and Ubering or Lyfting everywhere, it is very easy to get stuck. My friend and I were waiting for our Uber for a good 20 minutes, and it never came. Right as we were about to get a Lyft, the park rangers came over to us and told us that the cars wouldn't be able to come up the hill because they had closed the gate. We either had to take a cab that was already up there, or walk down to meet it. They claimed it was a 20 minute walk. They lied. It was about an hour downhill, walking in the fog. My fellow intern and I talked the whole way down. My teammate and I were hitting the road the next day. We talked about our fears, excitement, nerves, hopes, and dreams about what the following months would bring. It was in these moments that part of the foundation of our friendship was laid.

In February of 2017, my teammate and I had a few days off in Portland, Oregon and were dying to go hiking. We hit the road with the hopes of making it to one of the big national forests right outside the city. Apparently, the forest was larger than we thought and closer to the city limits than we thought. We ended up crossing a bridge into Washington, driving around the mountain, going into less than 30 degree weather and were not dressed appropriately and then continued back over the bridge into Oregon once more and hiked alongside some train tracks in mid-calf deep snow.

In March of 2017, my teammate and I were stuck in traffic coming home from one of our presentations. We rolled down the windows, turned up the radio, and just started dancing. It was pure fun. Our sides were hurting after from so much laughter, but it was one of those moments you will always remember.

In March of 2017, my teammate and I were staying in the Muir Woods at a hostel that didn't have really good WiFi. As part of our internship, we needed to do a lot of online work, emailing and collecting data, all the not-as-glamorous moments of life on the road. I talked with one of the guys at the front desk to see where the best WiFi in Sausalito was, he said the NoNameBar right on the main road. Guess what we did that night? We went to a bar to get WiFi to email our home office, plan out our next week, and email students. We laughed, met some cool people, and got some delicious food. We watched the sunset over the bay. It was one of the most peaceful moments of our entire tour.

Something that is so amazing about all of these moments and many more that I hold so close to my heart is that I didn't Instagram, Facebook, or Tweet them. These were moments where I was so in the moment that I didn't take a photo to remember them later. Sure, at times I kind of wish I had. I wish I had actual documentation to remember what was said on the cold January night where a friend and I grew so close walking for an hour or more and then chasing down our Uber to get back home.

Sure, I wish I had some photos to remember the funny dance moves, carefree moments, delicious food that was eaten, but I don't.

Sure, I wish I had a few quotes written down from jokes that were said on the balcony, on the mattresses that were on the floor, but I don't.

These are some of the most memorable moments of life, and they're not found on social media, no matter how hard you scroll through my photos. Every moment doesn't have to be shared to get likes; sometimes it's the moments that we don't share that mean the most to us.

Chapter Thirty-Seven
Don't Just Talk, Do

If you can't tell already, I am a *dreamer*. In all interpretations of the word, I *love* to dream. When I dream, I *dream*. I didn't just dream of being famous when I was little, I dreamed of being the next Britney Spears. I didn't just dream of traveling to England, I dreamed of traipsing across all of the United Kingdom, Europe, and all the other continents.

I love it. It keeps my soul alive. But, I don't always put my dreams into practice.

Right before I turned 24, I really sat down and thought about myself and all that I am. *What do I want this next year of life look like? What do I want to be like in five years? Who do I want to be? What do I want to say I learned this year? Where do I want to go?*

These weren't tangible answers. It wasn't a math equation that would get me a beautiful, simple, rounded number like 2+2=4. These answers were more complex.

I started looking at my friendships, and I saw that I wanted to deepen them. I wanted to know that my friends were going to be my friends until distance or time or space or life wore us down. I looked at my hobbies and thought about what new skills I wanted to learn. I looked at my job and thought about how I wanted to stay where I was for the time being but grow within the company. I thought about countries I wish to visit in my twenty-fourth year. I thought about who I am as a person and what attributes I like about myself and where I needed some work.

I set to work on myself in my twenty-fourth year.

Every year before this one, I would often think about what I wanted the next year to bring but never actually followed through. It's like New Year's Resolutions, you and your friends make them and talk about them the weeks leading up to the New Year, and at the party you resolve to enjoy the last of your binging on eating *all* the cupcakes because come the New Year, you're going to eat them in moderation.

January 1st rolls around and you do well, because well you're in a sugar coma from the night before.

But come the second week of January, and I'm eating candy corn like I'm an addict, because well I am.

I wouldn't stick with my resolutions or what I wanted to change. I would work towards them and then decide how much I really loved cupcakes or brownies or candy corn or doughnuts and how my love for them surpassed my love for being healthy.

As I've grown older, my resolutions have changed to be more wholehearted, much like how I started looking at my twenty-fourth year. I want to work on myself as a whole, I want to know that the person I am today is going to continue to grow and become an even more interesting, intelligent, confident woman. I'm stuck with me for the rest of my life so I want to enjoy myself.

Here's to 24, a year of not just dreaming about what I want to do and who I want to become, but a year of actually working towards it.

As I type this, I am two months into being 24, and let me tell you, there are days where all I want to eat is donuts and coffee, but I only eat one and then eat a banana too. There are times when I don't want to sit down and write because all that will come out is gibberish, but I sit down and try. There are times where I really don't want to go for a walk or run or bike ride, but I force myself to go because I'm stuck inside all day, and I need some vitamin D. There are days that I just want to buy everything at Target, but I do try some clothes on and just don't buy them because I have student loans that need to be paid off.

These changes aren't anything major, it's not a giant axis tilt from one side to the other. It's a slow turn to become what we one-day hope to be.

Chapter Thirty-Eight
Failure

I want to share with you a really amazing story about my life.

The summer before my junior year of college, (Yes, THAT summer where pretty much my whole life changed.) I was working down on my school's campus as a summer student custodian, working as an event staffer, and taking an accelerated chemistry course and statistics online. It was a busy summer to say the least.

One day while I was taking a small break from vacuuming a dorm common area, I got on my phone and pulled up Twitter. Twitter is one of my favorite social media platforms. I'm not entirely sure why, but I think the way to connect easily with others both near and far and see what they are doing with their lives intrigues me.

As I was scrolling through my newsfeed, I saw this incredible quote by someone named Caleb Stanley that had been re-tweeted by someone I follow. As I read the tweet, I knew right then, this person must be an author and that I have to read his books. His words were so profound and truth filled I wanted to know more. I clicked the tweet and went to Caleb's profile, where I found out he was not an author but instead one of the co-founders of a worship movement in Georgia called The Alternative.

When I clicked the link to The Alternative, my heart pulled in my chest, this was something I wanted to experience. This was something that would set my soul ablaze. This was something for me.

The Alternative was working to create a community of faith, a place of worship for people of all walks of life to come to, a place where you can come and be who you are and be changed by Jesus and change others as a result. It seemed perfect.

Except that it was in Georgia and I was in Indiana.

A few days went by, and I continued to think about the Alternative. It seemed too good to be true, but I still just knew, deep down, that I needed to go.

So I decided to put it to the test. *Ok Jesus, if you want me to go so badly, someone has to go with me. There's no way I can do that drive by myself, plus Mom and Dad won't let me. And too, what about a car? My car won't make it there.*

I started to message *tons* of friends, telling them about this amazing organization and worship night that was coming up in just a few weeks. It was a blanket message, but I sent to it anyone who I thought would have even the slightest interest in going.

Everyone said they were busy that weekend but it did sound fun and wished me luck on finding someone to go with.

I had told my friend Ashley about it since the beginning. We both have a similar dream of starting something like this in Indy, a way of connecting the many churches that excelled at different things and reaching different people all in one common place, worship. It was a dream I had when I started college, and I still hold it in my heart today.

She was interested in going just as much as I was, our only problem was work and transportation. We could do it cheap, we lived off of PBJs anyway.

A week before the event, we both got our work schedules, which neither of us had asked off for that weekend, leaving it up to God to show us that this was what we needed to do. We both had the weekend off. Saturday and Sunday.

We knew we had to go.

I sent an email to The Alternative's questionnaire asking if it would be possible to talk with the organizers of the event. We were curious how it all started and honestly how we could potentially branch out in the north. We wanted to know more than just what was on the website.

The weekend came, and we left at the crack of dawn. The drive was only supposed to take 9-10 hours at the most. Thanks to construction we were on the road for 15 hours and barely made it to the venue for the start of the worship night.

That night was one of my most favorite nights.

Ashley and I were exhausted from having just driven so much. We were a bit hungry. But we were excited, and that excitement kept us going. We knew something important had led us here to this moment.

The worship was indescribable, everything we needed to hear. We let our guards down and heard more clearly from the Lord than we ever had.

Our original plan was to arrive into town early and find a hotel for the night. Since we arrived just minutes before it all started we were homeless when we met all the organizers and they offered to let us stay in their home. They were incredibly generous in taking care of us that weekend, cooking for us, paying for meals, and praying over us. They even let us pick their brains on all that they had gone through to start and how they got involved.

It was magic.

When Ashley and I got home, we knew we wanted to start something similar. We didn't know how or what, but we wanted to.

We started reaching out to all our musically talented friends. We went to church after church to see how everyone worshiped, what we saw people partake in and what we didn't. We prayed and listened and sought council and finally the day arrived. We found the place for the first worship night, a friend's apartment. We found people to help lead worship. We invited all our friends to come. There in the sweltering August heat, on the evening of my 21st birthday, 15 of us worshiped in my friend's apartment.

It was magic once more.

There was something eye-opening about how long it took us to get everything set up and put together, just to tear it all down from my friend's living room in less than two hours. But we had done it; we had our first worship night.

The next month came around and my life started changing with applying for the World Race, but still we found our second location, the evening before our worship night. It was bigger, more grandeur, we wanted to fill the seats with everyone.

5 of us came out.

It was still magic. It was short and sweet but so good.

As my life was changing with preparing to go on the Race and still finish out my semester, I put the worship nights on hold. I had one more as a fundraiser to get onto the field but that was the last one.

The flame for creating a community that lived to worship and connecting with one another dimmed as other things took center stage in my life.

Fast forward a few more months to when I came home from the Race and began my life back in Indiana. I met up with some friends from school and one mentioned the worship nights that I had started, *"Gwen are you going to do those worship nights again?" "Oh yeah, whatever happened with those?"*

I could feel my face flush red with embarrassment. Here I was, having been blessed to do so much, having encouraged others to dream big dreams, to take small steps toward them, when I myself had let dreams die away.

I'm not sure if I will ever continue with planning worship nights. I think they are wonderful, and I encourage as many of you as possible to go and check out The Alternative. They are an incredible group of young people working to change the world one life at time. Whether or not you can go, I would encourage you to attend or even plan your own worship night if you can.

I planned some. I dreamed big, big dreams of connecting the north side to the south side and every soul in between in my city with one common event. I wanted it to last; I wanted it to still be alive today.

Perhaps one day, in the distant or not-so-distant future, these worship nights will continue, I honestly don't know.

But one thing is for sure, I am so happy I tried. I am so happy that I chased after this dream if only for a little while. I am so happy that I can say I did it.

Now when I think of these worship nights and what has come from them, my face no longer flushes with embarrassment and hopes the subject will change quickly. My eyes tend to water a bit, and I get a far-off look remembering what was and what just may come to be.

It's ok to fail, it means you tried.

Chapter Thirty-Nine
Childlike

Do you remember growing up how a simple blanket suddenly became a fort or an airplane or a ship? Anything could be anything; *you* could be anything. We used our imaginations for everything as we were younger, and I thought it was the coolest thing.

I love our imaginations. I love how everyone can look at, well, anything and see something different. It's beautiful how we are all made the same but work so differently.

Something that I really love is how a young child's mind works. Take my nieces for example: Day in and day out, they play games. Some of the most absurd games that don't really make any sense in my mind. One of their favorites right now is the "Boat Game," where we sit on the floor with my legs stretched out and they sit in between them like they are on a boat. Pretty simple right?

I sway my legs back and forth like we are rocking on the water. Still simple and fun right? *Then* one of them jumps out of the boat (my legs) into the water (on to the carpet) and starts to swim after their lost tiara. Or off to go see the mermaids.

This is where I smile.

When I was five or three or even seven, I probably played a game similar to this, although many of the games I played when I was young consisted of me flying, not swimming, but still.

My nieces are able to envision this alternate world where I am a boat. They're swimming after their lost tiara and talking with mermaids. It's beautiful.

Their minds are so intricate, so pure, that they can imagine anything.

As we grow older, the imaginative parts of our brains lessen. I'm sure this has something to do with being more aware of how the world *actually* works. Like when you realize you have to make money in order to spend money. I think that as children, we are able to see the world a certain way, almost as though we have a veil over our eyes. We can't see *everything;* we only see what we want to see, or choose to see. As we grow older though, this veil begins to lift as we learn more about life. We see that legs are just legs, not a boat.

But here's what I think, I think we can choose whether the veil stays on our eyes or not.

A few days ago I got a bike. I paid $50 for it at a garage sale. Steep yes, but in wonderful condition. I haven't ridden a bike since a rode a tandem one in Honduras a few years ago. Riding my bike now is glorious. I rode it all the way home from across the neighborhood.

It was so easy to get back on the seat and pedal away. How I love the feeling of the breeze on my face and whipping my hair behind my head. I felt like I was flying.

As I rode back home, I laughed and smiled, I was so *happy* at something so simple, I felt like a child.

As we grow older, we have more responsibilities; we have more things we have to worry about. *Is my paycheck enough to make it for another two weeks? If I eat out today, can I still go see that movie? Can I make that payment? I have to make time to do my laundry. Don't forget about your emails! I need to email back so-and-so.*

We tend to lose sight of the small things because we are so future-focused. It's fair; our lives revolve around more than just playing games. But when we begin to lose sight of the small things, the "stop and smell the roses" moments, I think this is where we allow the veil to be lifted. We no longer see a blanket as a fort, a cape, or an airplane; we see it as a blanket, an object to keep us warm. What would happen is we allowed ourselves to be children again? How much would our lives change?

I think we need to give ourselves grace to be kids. To have fun, laugh deep, belly-aching laughs, ride our bikes for fun rather than exercise, eat ice cream for dinner, spent the entire day in our pajamas reading a book, maybe even make a fort of two, and pretend to be living in the Middle Ages, or monkeys in the forest. When we allow ourselves to be kids again, our lives get brighter.

God calls us to be children, to have faith like children. I didn't always understand what this meant until my nieces got older. My nieces trust me not to drop them when I swing them around in my arms. My nieces trust that when we make them dinner, it will be food they enjoy and will fill them. My nieces trust me to take care of them, to fight off the bad guys, to run faster to catch them, to help them swim not sink. As adults our minds rationalize everything, "if we do this, we'll get this" kind of outcome. It becomes a math problem. To children, it just is.

As I was riding my bike that day, I realized just how simple and easy it is. Sure faith can be a bit more complicated. But what if it wasn't? What if faith was just like my nieces using my legs as a boat, pretty simple? What if we allowed ourselves to be children once more, not only in our lives, but in our faith? I think the world could truly change.

Chapter Forty
Like the Clouds

I remember when my friends and I would spend hours outside looking up at the sky and trying to find shapes in the clouds. The most popular ones that greeted us were elephants and dragons and dolphins. We would wave "Hello" before they drifted off to go greet others that were watching them.

Somehow as my friends got older, they stopped looking for the clouds in the sky to wave to as we were passing by underneath them. I, however, didn't. I kept watching the clouds, mesmerized by the way they would form, bending with the wind and stretching as far as the eye could see.

It struck me just a few days ago while I was outside on my break, watching the sun come up and the clouds begin to wake, how no two clouds are the same, much like a snowflake.

I have been blessed to see clouds in all the hemispheres, North, South, East, and West. Some days they looked just like clouds. Others, the sun's reflection on them reminded me so deeply of home that my heart ached. Others too, I would glance up and hardly see one in the sky, and it felt like I was in another world.

Clouds are like people: some clump together, others drift apart. Some even take different shape than their original one. I think clouds are like dreams too. Sometimes when we're young, our dreams take a certain shape. For me, I dreamed of being a famous singer, and then a teacher, of being the next Beethoven or YoYoMa. Now, I dream of surfing, of sun, of adventure, of more stamps on my passports. I dream of running a coffee shop. I dream of getting to write and share more of my story with others. I dream of listening to others' stories and getting the privilege of sharing their story with others.

Perhaps we all at one point dreamed of graduating high school, getting into college, of excelling in college and finding our passions. Maybe we all have dreamed of falling in love and getting married. Some of my friends have achieved this beautiful dream and others are still off floating trying to decipher what theirs is now.

My dreams have changed over time, much like my friends' dreams. Sometimes all our dreams clump together, and we encourage one another in them. We are all dreaming of getting healthy and fit for Kierstin's wedding coming up. Rachel and I both dream of starting the day with the Lord.

Just like when we were kids, not everyone saw the same thing in a cloud. We would argue for a few minutes on whether or not it really *was* an elephant or actually a ferocious lion stalking its prey. Or maybe even it was an opera singer or a coach and buggy. No matter what it was, we all saw some kind of beauty in the clouds.

When it comes to our dreams, we all see different aspects of them. When my nieces dream of being princesses or fairies, I see a beautiful imagination that is taking shape. I also wonder and worry slightly if they will be the young girls who hate getting dirty while we play in the yard and feel like they have to wait for Prince Charming to be able to do something.

When Kierstin tells me her dream of being a physical therapist, I am so happy for her and can see her sitting with her patients in their rooms working on their stretches to help better themselves. I also see the *years* of schooling and the debt and the struggle. But I know that if she sets her mind to it, she can do it.

With Sara dreaming of being a stay-at-home mom, I wonder what will come of her love of dance. And yet, here is she teaching dance at church and to her daughters and her sister-in-law. How perfect.

We all see our dreams usually just in one way. I dreamed of being a famous singer when I was five. While I never (or haven't yet, you never know) toured the world performing for hundreds of thousands of people, I've been able to sing in multiple choirs all across the state.

While I have never been a teacher in the traditional sense, I have been able to share things I've learned with those around me.

While my piano skills are about on par with my youngest niece, I will by no means be playing at the next symphony, but my love for music has continued in my adult life.

When we look at our dreams, they don't always come out to be the beautiful elephant that we first saw, sometimes they really do end up being the opera singer, or a lion stalking its prey. We just might have to turn our heads and squint a bit.

No matter how small a dream is, it could just be like one of those wispy clouds that scatter the sky on a clear fall day. They can easily become a larger rain cloud; they just have to find the ones that will propel them forward to their dream, to their passion. Soon you'll be raining down on us, dancing, as all of your dreams coming true.

Chapter Forty-One
YOLO Mentality

We live in a culture full of acronyms: YOLO, TBH, SMH, HMU. Some of which, if I'm being totally honest, I don't even know what they mean, and I end up having to search them online to understand the meaning.

I'm not sure when it happened, perhaps it was the era of Instant Messaging when we all started abbreviating our sayings, or maybe it was even sooner. But there's something really interesting about the change in the way we all start to use shorthand phrases.

I remember a ton of crazy phrases that my friends and I said over the years. We would refer to one another by just our first initial in actual conversations like we did in text messages. We would say LOL out loud and OMG. We even said, "Wpazzuuuup" in the early 2000s. There are tons of different vernaculars to emphasize different parts of our sentences. One of the best acronyms that came out of a song, I think, was YOLO: You Only Live Once.

Or perhaps more accurately: You Only Have Today.

That's been the way I have tried to live my life these past few years, living for the moment. It's an important message, especially to someone like me who cannot wait for the next thing to come my way. I *love* looking at all the possibilities of my future with what and where I could end up. It's intoxicating and mysterious and attractive to me. I want to know all my options, and I wonder where I will be this time next week, next month, next year. But it's also a dangerous mentality, because it takes my eyes, mind, and spirit away from the now, today.

When I start to think about YOLO, I try to ignore all the negative thought processes that come with an easy excuse to do something stupid with the thought that "I only live once." and now I look at it with the idea of, "What am I living for today?"

When you live for the moment and each day of your life, you live for what you love.

What do you love?

There's this wonderful quote by Rumi, "Respond to every call that ignites your spirit."

What ignites your spirit?

For me, it's Jesus, travel, and sharing love.

These three things alone are not a job, or even really a livelihood. But together, they could be, there's a possibility I can do all of these and many more in my lifetime.

You see, we aren't called to be *'normal'*. We're called to be ourselves.

If we were all the same, can you imagine how boring that would be? Everyone parted their hair exactly the same way. Everyone had the exact same hair color, eye color, and skin color, taste in clothes. There would be no more shopping in your friends' closets because you all had the same stuff. We would no longer be able to learn something from our friends or family because we all have the same ideas and same thoughts.

Can you imagine that? Personally, I think that would be unbelievably boring. We are all meant to be different people, the person that God has created us to be.

There are certain societal rules and expectations that are put on us from an early age. I have felt them, worked within them, achieved some, and ran from others. I did not realize just how many there were until I learned them in a script for my internship:

"We are born. We go to school. We go to school to get good grades. We get good grades to get into a good college. We get into a good college to get more good grades. We get more good grades to get a good job. We get a good job so we can buy some really cool stuff, and then we buy that really cool stuff so we can die. That's it." [2]

_____

2 All credits of this quote are from Thirst Project

When I read these words, something clicked. I don't want my life to just be good grades, money and things. I want it to be *something more.*

At these words in our presentation, we would invite students into something more, and that is what I want to invite you into. I want to invite you into taking the road less traveled, the option that isn't what everyone wants to do, the not-normal way of living, and all those other Pinterest-able quotes.

Live in the moment. Live in the now. You only have one life, so live it the way that you want to and not the way someone else wants you to be.

It's hard, it won't be all rainbows and butterflies, but it will be so, so worth it.

Chapter Forty-Two
Dream a Story

I was recently presented with a challenge: creating a "single life" bucket list. All the things that I wanted to do before I tied the knot.

Easy right? Not really. I want to do hundreds of things in my life, and I struggled with finding a way to decide what I wanted to do before I was married and what I wanted to do afterwards.

Then it hit me, *What do I want to be able to share, to show this great story to tell people, potentially my future husband, that I've been able to do?*

That's when I realized what we all dream of doing:

We are meant to do more with our lives than get good grades, get into a good school, find a wonderful job that pays the bills, get married, have children, buy some really great stuff, and then we die.

We are meant to do so much more than this. We are meant to dream, to live each day to the fullest, to achieve goals, to save money, to spend that money on things that we love, not just bills we have to pay. We are meant to live this life wonderfully; after all we only get one.

So what kind of life do I want to live? What do I want to have in my story?

These were the questions that began to form in my mind. I started to dream again. I started to realize just how many things I want to do. Some were small, like travel up to Michigan for a day and see the cute little towns, take a girls' trip with some of my best friends, spend New Year's somewhere amazing like on the beach somewhere. Some were a bit larger, like publishing this book that you're holding, open a coffee shop, hike the Camino de Santiago, learn French, travel across Europe, go to Vancouver, write stories of people I've been able to meet. The list goes on and on.

You know one of the reasons why we love movies or books? It's because the story captivates us. Two of my favorite shows are *How I Met Your Mother* and *Friends*. They're classic shows! You get invested in the characters and want to know what they decide to do. You see their development, how they change and find new passions, how they work through the hardships of life. You're rooting for them; you want them to succeed (at least most of the time).

That's how we are in our lives too. When I have a friend tell me about a hardship they are facing, I am holding their hand every step of the way. Do they need a distraction? Bring on the food and games! Do they need someone to grab tissues, wine, and ice cream? Give me ten minutes, and I'll be there. Do they just want to know that someone is right there for them? Me, my sweet friend, I'm right here, and I'll always be here, holding your hand during the good, the bad, the ugly, and the beautiful. When someone tells me about a new opportunity, I am chanting their name on the sidelines. I'm holding the "You Go!" sign as they walk into their new job. I'm offering my car to help them move, my time to help them succeed. Whatever it is that they need, I am there.

I want my friends to succeed in their lives, and I want to succeed in my own. I want to be able to have this beautiful story, one that blows my mind with all that I have been able to do in my life. One where when a new opportunity comes, I don't just think it's anything, but I am able to realize just how much of a gift it is for me to be able to have it. I want to live a life where I see just how wonderful each blessing is that comes my way. I don't want to ever realize that it's 'normal' to have this or that. I want to be in awe of it.

I want to live a life where I tell my nieces about the time that I backpacked across Spain, hardly knowing any Spanish besides "Please" and "Thank you", "Hello" and "Goodbye", "Where's the bathroom?" and "Sorry."

I want to tell them about the time that I raced out of work after my shift into a car of expectant friends to go on a weekend road trip.

I want to tell them about the time I hopped on a plane to go surprise a friend for their birthday.

I want to tell them about the time I lived abroad, how I made friends, how I worked.

I want to tell them about the time that I worked so hard, poured my heart out into words and got to share my story with everyone.

I want to tell them about the time that I *finally* stood up on a surfboard for the first time.

The list is endless.

When I started to look at the stories that I wanted to be able to tell, I realized how I wanted to live my life. And although I am not *the* Author, I am a moving piece, one that gets to have all of these amazing adventures. One that loves to travel, one that loves to meet new people, one that loves to share the stories of those that she met along the way.

No one's story is the same either. Some friends dream of telling the story of how they met their other half in school and have been inseparable ever since. Some friends dream of finding the perfect job, one where they can use all of their talents. Some friends dream of being parents. Some friends dream of seeing the stars.

Everyone has a different passion, a different story. But we all have one thing in common: we want to live a story, one that is worth reading and worth telling. So why not dream up one and star in it?

Chapter Forty-Three
Give Up the Wonder

It started with a simple Google search. I was reading over an article that I was writing for an online magazine on travel. It seemed pretty much ready to send out, so I brought up the internet to send it away to my editor and decided to search it: "Jobs at the New York Times."

I felt a little silly; who I am but a twenty-something who dreams of writing one day for real? Who am I to get hired at the *Times—the Times* for crying out loud? I don't even have a journalism degree. Who I am for them to even look at?

There it was: an editorial writer was being hired, three actually. I read the job description, and it sounded amazing. I would be able to write about pretty much anything I wanted to. I could do a series, how cool would that be?! I could do combined pieces with other writers. I could write about anything that I wanted: policy, humanitarian work, the environment, even lifestyle pieces, or all of it combined.

I clicked the application and as the site loaded, and my hand hovered over the "x" to close the screen.

What am I doing? Why in the world would the Times *want to hire me? What do I have to offer? I don't have a journalism degree. I blog and write for an online magazine. There's probably hundreds of grammatical errors and spelling mistakes in my work.*

Panic and uncertainty swirled in my mind.

Then a small bit of wonder began, *What if I just waited for a few more months. I just got promoted, how rude would it be if I left right away? What if I wait until my book is done too? Then I would be able to share that I do know a bit more of what I'm doing. What if I just focused on the work I'm already working on? When I go to bed tonight, will I wonder about this job? Will I wonder about it in a few months? I don't want to be working at Starbucks forever, could this be my way out? Will I wonder about this moment for months, years to come? Do I want to wonder? Or do I just want to know?*

I realized that I didn't want to be filled with the "What if's", the "wonder" of what could be with this job opportunity. I didn't want to just wonder what it may be like to apply at the *Times* or for a magazine I dream of working for or even a company where I would love to be employed. I wanted to *know* that I did it.

My resume is extremely colorful. It's one where the only consistent themes are coffee, travel, and Jesus. Much like the rest of my life. While these are incredibly important themes, there's a larger one, the neglect of *wondering*. Whenever I begin to look for a new job opportunity, I do so with the thought that I will at least try. For many of us, the fear of failure of missing out on a different opportunity is what drives many to stop in their pursuit of something that could set their soul ablaze. But not me. I dream of those oddities that I am in no way truly qualified for, but where I will thrive.

These pages hold many of these moments and even more. The past years of my life have shown me that the when I disregard the fear of the unknown, the fear of *wondering*, and I just do, the outcome is so much greater than I ever imagined.

As I laughed my way through the application, it was one of the most joyous moments of my life. Sure, will the *Times* choose a twenty-something blogger and aspiring journalist to be an Editorial Writer? Probably not, but I tried didn't I?

As I laid in bed that night, my mind swirled with thankfulness. I didn't have to wonder what it might be like days, months, or years down the road had I not applied. Nor if I was searching for the best moment to apply. I *did* apply. I took the chance. It was scary, it was uncertain, but I did it.

Chapter Forty-Four
Can I Do This?

I woke up this morning wondering about all that I had done and then where I am now. I wondered if I could ever go back.

Not to the person that I was, or necessarily the circumstances, but the adventures. *Could I actually go and do mission work again? Could I live with just what I was able to put into my backpack? Could I go back to traveling the world? Could I go back to proclaiming the name of Jesus Christ and His love to the lost, the broken, and the weary?*

At times, I want to so desperately. I want to part ways with comfort that I have grown so used to here and go back to the basics where all I have is literally on my back, and all I know that is coming is what I have been told.

Something changes in being home. My comfort has become something that I almost hold like I don't deserve, something that I don't want, but at the same time am afraid to let go of.

I wonder if I can truly go back to the ways I used to live. *Do I still hear God's voice when He has a word? Would I still feel that thumb in my back that is telling me this is my chance? Will I still take the chance? Will I still discern? Will I still know?*

You know how when an athlete takes a season off to rest or explore something else, they still have to train, because if they don't, their muscles will atrophy? The same thing happens to us. If we don't continually use our physical and spiritual muscles, they will atrophy. I don't want that. I don't want my spiritual muscles to die. I don't want to grow limp.

Here I am, trying to grow where I am planted. I go to bed at 8pm and wake up at 6am. I stay at home mostly, going out to see friends or try a new coffee shop. The last major travel I did was *ages* ago, and while

I miss it, I look for more reasonable hours of flight times, even if they are a bit more expensive. I like the comforts I have, but I am in no way *uncomfortable.*

I don't want to be uncomfortable where I am. Sure, I like some of the comforts of where I am. I *love* having a bed, a bathroom, running water, electricity, and entire closet of my own. I do. I love it and don't want to get rid of it. But I'm scared to put down roots where I am, simply for the fact that I *may*, one day, be called away.

To some it may sound crazy, but to my heart and soul that long for more, it makes perfect sense.

I long to feel the fire inside me roar once more. It is a burning hearth that sways as the breeze rolls by.

I long to feel the sand between my toes and the sun on my face and the water lapping against my body.

I long for the days to be full of laughter and pure wonder and to get hugs full of deep love.

I long for these days, even though I am more scared than I can put into words.

I long to know that my life isn't just here but that my life is all over, being touched by hundreds of other souls, other stories. I long to hear God's name praised in all languages, all areas, all regions of the Earth.

I long for these while I still wonder how they can actually happen, if they will. I long for so much and, God willing, it will all happen.

But I do indeed wonder if I even can still.

As these all swirl in my mind, I am reminded that anything God calls us to, we can do, with Him at our side.

Perhaps one day, He will call me again, just as He called the rich, young ruler, to give up all his possessions and follow Him. For me, I hope and pray that day is not a hard decision. I hope that I have not let the comforts of home distort what I am truly called to do. I hope that I no longer fear roots being created for fear of leaving, but instead enjoy the time that I have here and make the most of it.

Chapter Forty-Five
Explore Your Own Backyard

One of the things I love about travel is that you don't always have to pull out your passports. Sure it's crazy fun to plan a trip across an ocean, think of all the beautiful sights you'll see, the languages you'll hear, the food you'll get to eat; but it's not always necessary.

One of my most favorite things to explore is my own backyard.

I've lived in the same city my entire life. My parents bought the house that I am currently writing in a few years after my brother was born and about a year before I came into the picture. It's my home. My room in my house has changed multiple times over the years, but it's still home.

My city has changed drastically over my 20-some years of life. Main Street went from two lanes to four; construction has abounded with new buildings, bigger schools, and larger highways; there are tens of thousands of more people here than were when I was young.

I love when new friends come to my town, some have even settled here long term. They tell me about all these things that are going on. Just a few days ago, Rachel and I were baking apple crisp to celebrate fall (even though it was about 80 degrees out.) She told me about movies in the park that were free! Festivals coming up, that were free! Did I know about these, did I want to go?

I had no real idea they existed. My mom informed me that yes, we used to go to those events when we were younger, but as we got older, we had more things going on. But I for the life of me, I cannot remember going to the park and watching movies on a giant screen. I can only recall scenes of *Gilmore Girls* when they did this in their small town.

When my itch to travel starts to come back, as much as I want to pack my bags and book a transatlantic flight, or go back to the West Coast and explore, I can't always do so financially. So instead, I get in my car, hop on my bike, to explore my own backyard.

There's tons of new restaurants popping up monthly all around my city. Hundreds of restaurants from tapas to burgers to beer to wine rooftop bars. I want to try them all.

Some days, I have little to no money and sometimes no one to go with, plus if I'm driving myself, do I really want to enjoy a glass of wine in the middle of the afternoon? No. So instead, I search for new coffee shops to try, maybe sit and read, maybe people-watch. Maybe even write a few more pages for you read.

There are tons of new parks coming into the area too, tons of days, worth of frolicking in the sun and grass.

Perhaps you no longer live in the town you grew up in. Have you ever gone back and explored?

I remember how every Thanksgiving growing up, while the turkey was cooking and all the sides had been made, my dad took my brother and I to different school playgrounds. The year we went to my soon-to-be middle school and played on that playground was probably my favorite. This was going to be my playground in just a few months.

Or maybe it was the time when my brother spun me around on some turning, twisting ride, and I got sick and couldn't eat much at dinner. Either way, I remember them both fondly.

One of these days, I want to take my nieces to these same playgrounds. To show them the slides their dad and auntie used to ride down with glee. To show them the baseball field where I got stung by a bee while running the mile. To show them the car that had been recreated into artwork by students before both their father and me.

I want to walk the same routes I used to walk to get to my best friends' houses when I was little. My how times have changed. Back then no one had a fence, and we could run the length of the block just through backyards to get to my house or theirs. I suppose taking the long way and actually using sidewalks is just as fun now.

There are countless ways to entertain ourselves wherever our feet are. Even when our souls long to be elsewhere—to go and explore the ruins of Pompeii, to hike the Appalachian Trail, to see Machu Picchu—there is still much more to explore in our own backyards than we will ever truly get to see.

Chapter Forty-Six
It's OK to Wander

One of the reasons why I love social media is because so many people post some beautiful reminders about some of the most successful people in the world reminding us that they weren't always successful.

Walt Disney was fired from the Kansas City Star because his editor thought he lacked imagination. He created the Disney empire.

Oprah was fired from her first television job as an anchor. Now she's, well, she's Oprah.

JK Rowling was a single mom living off of welfare when she created Harry Potter.

Want to know why I find these reminders so beautiful? At the moment, my life is made up of short-term goals, ones that are achieved in mini milestones. Those milestones are graduating high school, getting accepted into college, going to college, graduating college, getting a wonderful job, finding the one you want to spend the rest of your days with, creating a life with them. These are all short-term things, but I don't think that our lives are always meant to be lived this way. I don't think that our lives are meant to be lived by graduating college and going directly into our dream job where we will stay for the rest of our lives, gaining a wonderful paycheck, having enough time to hang out with friends, maybe even starting a family.

I think that life is beautiful and yes, it does sometimes happen for some people this way. But it's not bad to go about life in the opposite direction.

Perhaps the major you received in college (or maybe you didn't even go to college) isn't at all where you are working now. Maybe you studied English and are working as a Vet Tech. Maybe you studied science and are working as a receptionist.

Me? I studied Environmental Sustainability and am currently working as a barista.

There's no real correlation, believe me. I just love coffee.

I say this with as much passion and sincerity as I whisper it to my own soul.

We don't have to figure our lives out right away.

We don't have to know what is next.

We don't have to be where all of our friends are.

We don't have to find 'the perfect job' or 'the one' right away.

We have permission to wander about in our lives. When we wander, we learn more of who we are as people. If I hadn't taken advantage of so many of the opportunities I had in college and right afterwards, I would be surprised if I even had a steady job. I think I would be even more antsy than I currently am, dreaming of the next place where I could go.

To be fully honest, I'm not sure if some people just figure it out faster than others, or if they just decide, *this is something that I can stick with for a while.*

I think it depends on the person. Some of my friends have *always* known exactly what they wanted to do, but I haven't.

It's in my story to wander a bit more than my friends do. No matter how cliché the phrase is from *Lord of the Rings,* remember sweet friends, just because we wander does not mean that we are lost. We just like to enjoy the sights that we see and experiences we can have en route to our next destination.

Chapter Forty-Seven
Step Out

When I look back on my life, some of the best decisions of my life were made when I took a leap of faith.

The time I applied for an internship even though I wasn't old enough.

The time I went to a church even though I didn't know anyone.

The time I talked with a barista at a coffee shop.

The time I told a guy I liked him.

The time I applied for the World Race.

The time I told my University President that I wanted to work with Thirst Project.

The time I asked for help with a resume.

The time I talked to a stranger on a plane.

There is something truly beautiful about taking chances. The chances I thought about here aren't anything major; they were just a small decision to do something different one day.

Probably one of my favorite moments where I took a small leap of faith was in November of 2017. I was heading to Washington, DC to see some friends. I Love DC, like literally capital "L" Love.

There's something about it that just makes my heart happy. Maybe it's because it's the first city I ever *really* lived in on my own. It's the first city I really learned to venture out on my own and explore for myself. It's a city that holds so many memories of growth and opportunities.

Whenever I come here, I promise you, I think a strange, different Gwen takes over me and wants to talk with every person I walk by and get to know them, their story, and how they ended up here.

Okay, okay, you're right; that's how I am all the time, but in DC, I act on it a lot.

So much so that one time I stayed about an hour after a coffee shop had closed because I was talking to a barista and getting to know their story. But I digress. This particular time going to DC was a bit different for me. Leading up to the trip, my plans had changed hundreds of times, I honestly had lost count of what and why I was coming out here.

To top off the craziness of plans, I was in a boot. The kind of boot that you have to keep your foot in because you sprained it. DC is a walkable city, has a wonderful transit system, and if you stay above ground and like fresh air and walking, you can see so many beautiful places.

Anyway, as I was getting on the plane, I was hoping my seat buddy wouldn't mind if I took the aisle, as much as I don't usually like it, I knew it would be easier with my boot to not have to squeeze into the window seat, no matter how much I loved the view. As I walked down the aisle toward my row, my seat buddy was already there and taking photos out the window.

I said, "Hi," and motioned that I was placed in the window and then stopped and said, "Do you want the window? You're more than welcome to have it! It'll be easier for me anyway."

The gentleman was slightly taken aback by the turn of events but was happy to move over. Once I wrestled my foot into the small space, I turned and saw the guy taking photos of the wing out the window. Jokingly I asked, "Snapchat or Instagram?"

And thus began one of the best plane rides I have ever been on. This guy works for the Environmental Protection Agency (EPA). For the entire hour-plus flight, I asked him question after question, everything from what his role is (He works with water conservation – I know right?!) to climate change, renewable energy resources based off of geography, the global water crisis, jobs, how he started working there. The list is endless.

I'm honestly surprised that he didn't politely tell me to be quiet, but I'm so thankful he let me ask so many questions.

As our flight neared DC, I thanked him for answering all my questions and delighting me in knowing that there are jobs out there in my field, some that even sound fun, or at least interesting. He graciously gave me his card, and I asked (not like I hadn't asked probably 101 questions already) if he was free the next day to grab coffee or maybe even let me see the building. He said to shoot him an email, and he would see if he could.

A few hours later, while sitting at my favorite coffee shop in the city, I emailed him, thanking him for his time, lending his thoughts and asking if he was free the next day. That next day, I got to go see *the* Environmental Protection Agency. I know.

I can still barely believe it. It was truly a dream come true. The architecture alone is something to gawk at, and when you think about all of the projects, people, and research that goes along inside the building, I was weak at the knees.

I think this story is honestly hilarious and is also my life in a snapshot.

If I had just nodded to the gentleman that motioned that my seat was the window, squeezed past him and into it, and then sat on the plane for over an hour listening to the podcasts I had planned on listening to during the flight, gotten off, and then seen my friends, I would have missed out on something amazing. I would have missed out on getting to talk to someone who has one of my dream jobs.

It's occurrences like this that make me realize just how much of an impact the small things can have on the larger picture.

Friend, step out today. Take one small chance. Say "Hi" to someone. Sit next to someone. Ask to share a table at a crowded coffee shop rather than leaving and doing your own thing. It's one small, little detail that can change so much.

Chapter Forty-Eight
Take a Leap

I'll never forget the times that I have taken a large leap of faith in life:

When I applied to college, when I applied to both my internships, when I applied for jobs but didn't get them, when I applied for a job that I wasn't qualified for, when I told a boy I liked him, when I told my parents I wanted to take a year off school, when I started writing full time, when I joined a gym.

Some of these leaps were tiny hops compared to others; some were easier than others; some I had tears streaming down my face while others I was grinning from ear to ear

I'll never forget when I told one of my best friends that I had feelings for him. It was *scary*, my hands were shaking, I didn't want to mess up, I didn't know how to put my feelings into words. But they were there and I knew it and I just knew I had to share with him.

The *day* leading up to my decision, I was talking to one of my best friends about it. She had been there by my side through it all and knew what I was feeling. She asked me *why* I wanted to tell him, what was I hoping to get out of it. My response went something like this, "You know, I have no idea what I want out of this. I'm not expecting a date or him to tell me he likes me either, I just *know* I want to be honest with where I am, and if things don't work out, if he doesn't want to stay friends, that's ok, but I don't think that will happen."

When I wrote in my journal about it later that night I described it as feeling as though I had climbed a tree. I was up high, looking over it all, a bit scared by the distance to fall, but I *knew, I just knew,* that I wasn't going to. I *knew* that I was really just taking a step to a different branch, to a different spot in our relationship.

It turned out he had no idea I was falling for him, but that was totally okay. We talked about it and said how we wanted to be a part of one another's lives and maybe one day something could happen.

Sometimes it truly is terrifying to share where you are with someone. I'll never forget the day that I told him, and the days leading up to it and afterwards. I was scared, my hands were shaking, I thought I might throw up a few times too. I was nervous. What if it all backfired, or worse yet, what if I chickened out?

I think the same thing happens to us when we're scared of taking a chance, taking a leap. It happens with my friends all the time. They're scared to leave a job that they have because they know what it entails. They know their paycheck is coming every two weeks. They know where their money goes. They know what's expected of them. When a new job opportunity comes their way, they don't take it because of the *unknown*.

It is so easy to be scared of it. It is so easy to be unsure of what is going to happen because we don't have crystal balls. We can't look into the future and know exactly what someone is going to say, how they're going to respond, what is going to happen if we try out for something new.

But we can know that sometimes, all we have to do is take a chance. There's a beautiful quote by Erin Hanson, *"What if I fall? Oh, but my darling, what if you fly?"*

I was so scared to tell him I liked him, I thought I might fall; though I didn't fly, I didn't fall either, and that, my friend, is a win.

I was so scared to apply for a job that seemed crazy for me, like the *New York Times*. I haven't fallen yet, nor have I flown, and that is a win.

I was terrified to apply for an internship at Thirst Project, but darling, I flew. I soared.

I was so nervous to apply to yet another college. I didn't want to get rejected once more, but I didn't. I soared through my four years there and learned so much.

My friend, don't be so afraid of falling that you miss out on an opportunity to fly.

Chapter Forty-Nine
You Have Potential

When I was in high school, I was really sick. So sick that I could barely go to school. When senior year rolled around, I had no idea if I was going to make it into college. My health was a major question, my grades were in the toilet, and it just didn't seem possible.

As my friends started to apply to college after college, write their essays, ask teachers for recommendations, I felt stuck. I knew a few teachers that I could ask for a recommendation but otherwise I didn't know what was going to happen.

On paper, I looked like a delinquent child who hardly ever went to school, who never cared about class nor the grades that I got, and lest I forget, my SAT scores, where it seemed like I only got the points for writing my name in correctly.

Then it hit me: on paper I don't look like any college would ever want me, so how can I persuade them to think differently? I can write about it.

I ended up writing a ten-page essay on myself and how I grew up and some of the struggles that I endured.

I told them what life was like growing up. I told them how I got sick. I told them what I missed and how hard I had worked to stay in school. I told them I wasn't really a delinquent—I just wasn't able to go to school all the time. I told them how when I started to get better, how it felt to walk outside again and feel the sun on my face without pain, laugh with friends, almost be normal.

I told them the passion that I had for being outside. The wise words that a dear friend said about how it's God's garden, and we are here to protect it.

How that was why I wanted to go to school. How I wanted the chance to study the environment to understand the changes that happened. To not only dream up solutions but to act on them.

Despite this paper, very few colleges saw my potential. The one that did put me on academic probation, which required I take *very* beginner courses. But they still let me in and welcomed me with open arms.

They saw my *potential*. And I am so thankful they did. Because I went to their school, I excelled in some classes, nearly failed others. I was helped, mentored, and shown so many options.

People believed in what I could do. They saw more than my toilet grades, they saw *potential*.

I know people saw my potential, but there was something different about this, they helped me achieve mine. They helped me begin to take the steps away from being a young girl who was sick all the time to a girl who could go to class and learn and dream of what she could one day do.

Honestly, I don't know where I would be if my university hadn't seen my potential. I know ultimately I would have ended up where God wanted me all along. I was so happy there. I met some life long friends. If no one has said it, I believe in you, I see your potential. Not who you once were, you're who you want to become.

Chapter Fifty

Be The Change

Let me share will you a little bit more about what it was like being sick during high school. Which if I'm being totally honest was a bit of a dream at first. I missed out on homework, exams and studying. But then it started to suck. I missed out on school dances, football games, movies, and parties.

When I finally started getting better at 17, I didn't know if I could graduate high school, let alone get into college, but I was determined to. My friends, parents, and mentors all encouraged me to apply to schools and see if I could get in, and me being my headstrong self, I was determined to. They also encouraged me to just be a kid and live life, From having lived a life full of doctor's offices, pain, and missed moments, I didn't want to miss out on anything else when I got better. I was determined to go back to school, to graduate high school and get into college.

You see, if someone told me at 17 that when I was 20, I would spend a semester interning in Washington, DC; at 21, I would travel the world and do mission work; at 22, I would get to go to England; at 23, I would travel across North America, speaking at middle schools, high schools, and colleges on the global water crisis, I honestly would have laughed and walked away. Gone and told my friends about some crazy person who thinks I can do more than just be a sick student who can barely understand math equations, nor whatever a mole is in chemistry.

But I didn't let myself keep that sick student label. I didn't let myself stay "a sick student." I woke up and realized, yes, I have been sick for the past few years of my life. And I'm bound to have good days and bad days. I'm not sure if I'll ever fully be healed, but I'm willing to take that risk. I'm willing to apply to schools and hope and pray that they will see my potential. I want to do more than just see doctor's offices; I want to see the world. I want to change the world.

I have been blessed to, and I know there is more to come.

You see, I didn't let my setback at 15 define the rest of my life.

Maybe you weren't sick growing up. Maybe you had a bad relationship, your parents split up, you failed a couple classes, you didn't get your dream job. I'll be honest, my heart breaks for you. Every little thing that didn't go perfectly for you, I'm sorry.

But you have a choice, just like I did at 17. You can choose each morning when you wake to either be the person you have been for your whole life and stay where you are, or you can choose to change.

I have to remind myself of this daily. There are times when I don't get the job I want, I'm not where I want to be in my life. But I've done some amazing things, and I know I'll keep doing amazing things.

I'm allowing my past to help drive me towards the future.

Will you join me? Because in the great words of Gandhi, "Be the change you wish to see in the world."

About The Author

Gwen Debaun is a Jesus-loving, coffee-drinking, adventure-seeking 20-something. You can often find her at a local coffee shop writing or reading, hanging out with her friends, or dreaming up her next big adventure. This is her first book, and she couldn't be more delighted to share it with you. She'd love to connect with you on social media and her blog. You can find her on Instagram @gdebaun12 and her blog at gwendebaun.wordpress.com.